INTRODUCTION

I T HAD BEEN A PARTICULARLY HECTIC DAY, and I was looking at the trellis on my deck when it hit me: all those obedient little wooden Xs lined up in straight rows were covered by wisteria branches that grew all over the place, up and down and sideways with abandon. My epiphany was brief: life will always be a lot. The wild, meandering wisteria running over and around the trellis was a picture of the way my life often feels—beautiful but also difficult to manage. It's not organized in predictable rows, uniform and orderly. It's unpredictable, moving in many directions at a time. It can be both dazzling and also a tangled mess at times.

Life will always be an unruly combination of responsibilities, relationships, interruptions, dreams, and drama, no matter what stage we're in. Part of that is God's good design, and part of it is the long shadow of sin that stretches all the way back to Eden. The good news is that it is right in the middle of this tangle of joy and strain that God wants to meet us. And he gave us the gift of his Word so we could know him and navigate life's challenges rightly. But how do we apply the Word to the full and varied lives we lead? How does it map on to our pressures and fears and busyness?

That's what this book is about—applying God-breathed words to our God-ordained moments and finding Jesus in them both. In these ten weeks, we'll explore biblical stories of people like us who had the same questions as we do.

TRISH
DONOHUE

YOU ARE
WELCOMED

DEVOTIONS FOR WHEN LIFE IS A LOT

New Growth Press, Greensboro, NC 27401
newgrowthpress.com
Copyright © 2023 by Tricia Donohue

Pattern Design: Tara Reed
Cover Design: Alecia Sharp
Interior Design and Typesetting: Alecia Sharp

ISBN: 978-1-64507-237-9 (Print)
ISBN: 978-1-64507-238-6 (eBook)

Library of Congress Cataloging-in-Publication Data on file

Printed in India

30 29 28 27 26 25 24 23   1 2 3 4 5

To Jim,

my first pick when life is a little and life is a lot.

CONTENTS

They were not model citizens who always got it right, but instead were real people who encountered an all-sufficient God in their weakness. Their imperfect but redemptive stories can encourage us in the middle of the strains, demands, and burdens we face. From these passages of Scripture, we can learn what it looks like to more fully depend on our heavenly Father and trust him more deeply, right in the middle of the chaos of our lives.

The chapter titles in this book are verbs—action words—which may seem exhausting at first glance. You might assume that getting help from God is hard work, but that's not true. God has done the work for us so that all we need to do is freely come to him—something we are curiously bad at doing. Jesus knew we were bound by sin so he took care of it for us on the cross, paying the debt we couldn't pay to fling the gates of heaven wide and present us to God in joy. The verbs that mark each chapter are invitations from our dear Father to live in the good of all that he is.

Would you like to put down your burdens and come to a God like that? The promise of the peace you can experience is as infinite as God's love. He welcomes you to come to him at every point in your life—at every turn, at every time—and he promises to receive you.

The format is simple. Each week we'll study a theme, passage, and character that together point us to God in a particular way. Reading the Scripture will be the key to understanding the material, so don't skip that part. God's words are better than my words. The questions offered at the end of each entry will help you to live what you learn and identify steps to real change. If you use this devotional five days a week, you'll be done in ten weeks, but you can go at whatever pace you like. There isn't a ribbon to run through at the end—just a Savior with open arms.

Come

A Follower's Frustration

A full life is a blessing, but the sheer volume of tasks, lists, and responsibilities can make that blessing feel like a burden. Stress smothers joy, and we wonder how to prioritize the God we love in the lives we manage. This week's readings show us a woman like us and the Teacher who loved her.

Deep and Wide

IDENTIFY

Which of the following feels overwhelming in your life right now: tasks to accomplish, emotions to manage, choices to make, or relationships to tend? Or is it all of the above?

IN THE TWENTY-FIRST CENTURY, flying should be easy: just board the giant jet that lifts you to the skies and soars like a falcon to your happy destination. But it's not. At times, it requires the multitasking skills of a circus performer.

Take, for example, going through security. Shoes off, laptop out, luggage lifted, children herded, conveyor belt stopped, suitcase searched, underwear out (why didn't I pack that on the bottom?), license dropped, people pushing, employee yelling—I get the sweats just thinking about it. And let's not even talk about boarding the plane with carry-on, coffee, purse, and—heaven help us—babies.

Whoever we are, sometimes life can feel like an international airport, as if we need an extra arm or extra brain to get anything done. Besides tasks to accomplish, we have emotions to manage, choices to make, and relationships to tend—often all at the same time. Even the starkest minimalist can't escape some of the complexities of life. If you're still unconvinced, here are a few more everyday zingers: Balancing the budget. Parking in the city. Working through conflicts. Navigating healthcare. Planning dinner menus for the month. I rest my case.

Some of the most frequent comments I hear from women are "I'm overwhelmed" or "I'm exhausted." Spiritual conversations share a similar tone: "My relationship with God is hard to fit in." "It's not super meaningful." "I'm stretched thin."

Thin. It's the word Bilbo the hobbit uses in *Lord of the Rings* to describe himself after carrying the burden of the ring for too long. "Sort of stretched. Like butter scraped over too much bread."[1] I've felt it. Have you?

Life can be a lot to handle, and some of that is our own doing. If we idolize productivity, saying yes to every extracurricular activity, fitness program, and business opportunity that comes our way, we may need to evaluate our priorities. But part of the fullness of life is also God's doing. He has placed us in a world dripping with stunning detail. Featured in the garden of Eden was a tree of life, not a rock or cube of life. A tree is a complex work of art. It moves. It grows. Its systems are so advanced that we can barely understand them, involving sunlight and water and minerals and magic. Its seeds house resurrection power. Both above and below the ground, trees are complicated, like the lives our Creator has entrusted to us—lives that reach and grow and move and bear fruit. A life meaningfully engaged with pursuing Jesus and loving others is rarely simple or tidy, but it certainly can be beautiful.

How do we, as limited human beings, live complex lives of wide responsibility without letting our souls grow thin? Today's reading in Psalm 36 tells us. We come to the deep one, whose love "extends to the heavens," and "faithfulness to the clouds," whose "righteousness is like the mountains of God," and "judgments are like the great deep." We come to the one who is everything we aren't, not only taking refuge in him but happily feasting on all his abundance and drinking from his river of delights.[2] If that sounds like a party, it is. He welcomes us to come to him for refreshment, abundance, and delight.

A song I sang in the kindergarten class of my childhood church sums it up: "Deep and wide, deep and wide, there's a fountain flowing deep and wide."[3] It's the fountain of life from Psalm 36, wide enough to cover all our needs, responsibilities, inadequacies, and sins, and deep enough to never run dry. Best of all, the fountain is found "with you," with God himself, and he beckons us to wade in.

The Christian life is not lived watching from the edges, being careful not to get wet. God invites us into a vibrant, interactive, personal relationship full of life and honesty and conversation. He knows who and how we are, loving us and calling us to love him in return. In fact, let's take a step into the fountain right now by asking God to show us more of himself through this study and to change us from the inside out.

Life does at times feel overwhelming, but when we step, then wade, then run into God's fountain of life, we find ourselves refreshed, splashing around in nothing less than the sheer delight of knowing him. What are we waiting for?

Does your soul feel "thin"? If so, what are the reasons for that?

_____

_____

_____

How can a full, complicated life be a beautiful one?

_____

_____

_____

Do you believe God can refresh you in his fountain of life? Ask him to do that for you this week, and jot down a verse from today's reading to review later.

_____

_____

_____

BELIEVE

Psalm 36:7–9: How precious is your steadfast love, O God! The children of mankind take refuge in the shadow of your wings. They feast on the abundance of your house, and you give them drink from the river of your delights. For with you is the fountain of life; in your light do we see light.

The View from a Window

Have you considered that productivity can be an idol when it promises peace and joy? Have you found that it delivers the joy it promises?

E LEARN ABOUT PEOPLE by the things in their houses. If you came to my house, you'd learn that I love throw blankets and hate clutter, and that I have kids who like to leave open bags of pretzels in the basement (don't ask me why).

We don't usually like people to observe what goes on within our walls without being invited, thus the invention of curtains and shades. We'd rather manage people's view of our lives, straightening cushions and refreshing our smiles. But sometimes God rips open the curtains before we're ready, and the spotlight shines straight on our least shareable moments. Readers have been peering through the window of Luke 10 into Martha and Mary's living room in Bethany for two thousand years, and it sheds some light on a struggle we all face.

As the curtain opens, we see Martha dashing around, dishrag in hand, glancing in irritation at her younger sister sitting cross-legged on the floor listening to Jesus with all the other guests. Martha feels anxious about all she has to do, and bitterness is brewing. She's stuck with all the work again, and Mary is sitting there with the visitors without a care in the world. As viewers, we feel the tension build, and our sympathies go out to this harried woman.

Jesus loved this little family with all their different personalities (John 11:5). We know that Martha, likewise, loved Jesus and welcomed him into her home, using her gifts of hospitality to bless the Teacher time and again. What a wonderful way to be remembered. We also know that after he came in, "Martha was distracted with much serving" (v. 40). She opened her door to Jesus but had a harder time enjoying his visit with all there was to do.

A friend and I lead an intro to Christianity course at a local drug rehab.[4] This week one of our discussion questions asked, "If you had an opportunity to meet Jesus, what would you say to him?" We all leaned back on the plastic chairs, trying to formulate thoughts appropriate for such an occasion. Answers were wistful. "I'd ask him why the road had to be this hard," one said quietly. Another decided she'd hug him. I'm still stumped after having led these conversations many times. I really don't know what I would say.

Poor Martha had this opportunity fall into her lap, and the first words the Bible records her saying to Jesus are a complaint. She's a firecracker with a lit wick when she approaches the Lord, blasting him not with questions or requests, but with accusations and orders: "Lord do you not care . . . ? Tell her then to help me." Martha carries wide responsibility and significant gifting, but she's thin in this moment: thin-skinned and thin-souled. The Son of God may have been enjoying pita chips in her living room, but she had a load of work to do, and Mary wasn't helping. Can a girl get a break? How do you commune with someone and serve him at the same time? How do we?

It's a real question. Christian women have plenty to do. Besides activities of family, work, and social lives, we have churches, devotions, and serving opportunities. Sometimes the sheer number of good things on our plates can feel counterproductive. But we can do it! We're strong, and if we eat right, organize well, drink coffee, and complain a little, we'll get it all done. At least that's what we tell ourselves.

Productivity has its place, but as we race through our agendas, do we enjoy God? Do we pursue worthy goals but not God himself? Do our friendships with others squeeze out friendship with Jesus? Is he sitting on our couch while we scurry around with checklists, complaining?

The familiarity of this story breeds oversimplification: Martha served too much, and that was bad so we should all be contemplative and sit at Jesus's feet all day. Parts of that conclusion are right and other parts are wrong, but it's a fast track to guilt and a real bummer if you are a doer type of person with a lot on your plate. Also, other parts of the Bible celebrate the kind of sacrificial service Martha gave, so what's the problem?

The crux of this little peek inside a home in Bethany is not that we should sit in a prayer closet all day and let our laundry grow mold. It's not that Type A people are shallow and inferior or even that Martha's busyness was wrong. Instead we learn that although there is always unfinished business, Jesus is what we need.

Because we need his perspective, we can prioritize his Word in the morning. Because we need his joy, we can sing to him as we drive to a meeting. Because we need his peace, we can give him our anxieties in the middle of the night. Because we need his love, we can breathe a prayer before a difficult conversation. He welcomes us to come again and again because the fountain won't run dry.

A thousand voices will tell us otherwise, but we need exactly what Martha needed. Let's put down our cutting board, our phone, or our keys and spend a few minutes talking with the Teacher who knows—and is—exactly what we need.

CONSIDER

In what ways can you identify with Martha as she prepares dinner? What questions or accusations might fly out of your mouth if you bumped into Jesus while you were in a stressful situation?

Like Martha, do you feel "distracted with much serving" while Jesus is in your living room? What are those distractions?

In what specific ways can you pursue Jesus today in the midst of unfinished business?

BELIEVE

Isaiah 26:3: You keep him in perfect peace whose mind is stayed on you, because he trusts in you.

The Good Portion

IDENTIFY

Which self-help strategies and books do you tend to rely on more than God and the Bible? What do they promise you?

THIS YEAR I switched from using a digital calendar to an analog bullet journal where one writes things down with a pen (gasp). In search of a simpler life, I predictably encountered the same complexities and lengthy to-do lists, just in handwritten ink rather than my iPhone font.

The reality is that we have a lot to do. Without shirking responsibility, there is no getting around busyness: You care for toddlers whose every step undoes what you do. You study for exams in challenging classes. You try to build, or at least keep, your friendships. You shop for your ravenous teenagers, go to work, and get the occasional much-needed haircut. And those are just the essentials!

The village of Bethany doesn't sound like a high-octane place, especially compared to our cars, schools, social calendars, and technological everything. But life in Martha's village may have been even busier than ours without all our modern conveniences. In any case, she was hosting the God of the universe for dinner. Talk about pressure. Martha is convinced that if Jesus just sees the scope of her need and the mess in her world, he will naturally agree with her assessment of what she needs—namely, relief in the form of Mary helping!

But Jesus's world is larger than the stage we play on, larger than the walls of our homes or the horizons of our towns, larger than our life spans and goals. His perspective takes into account eternal realities outside our current experience, and from this, he tells us a larger truth. That truth, written in the words of the Bible and the walls of our consciences, can feel jarring, but reality often is.

"Martha, Martha," he says, understanding her completely. "Trish, Trish," I mentally translate, "you are anxious and troubled about many things, but one thing is necessary. Mary has chosen the good portion, which will not be taken away from her" (vv. 41–42).

"The good portion." This phrase stems from a Hebrew word that refers to one's lot in life.[5] Jesus is saying that Mary had options and chose the right door, the best part of life. She chose him.

Jesus just accomplished in one phrase what an entire shelf of dog-eared books in my town's library can't quite pin down: How do we pursue the best in life? The shelf is real, and I've stood before it many times, mostly because even though I know the answer, the titles exercise a strange gravitational pull on me. It's probably that they all offer a "secret" or "key" or some other magical recipe for a bowl of euphoric fulfillment with a slice of wealth for dessert. But the messages on that shelf never really deliver on their promises. Readers are left empty because they haven't read Luke 10 where the good portion is revealed: be with Jesus.

The story merits slowing down and picturing ourselves in this scene. When we, like Martha, are stressed out and slogging through a jumble of responsibilities or emotions or temptations, what do we consider "the good portion" at that moment? Personally, what I want is to get this situation under control right now (cue bossiness) or to leave it behind (cue escapist phone usage). But my knee-jerk responses keep me from the answer I desperately need: the good portion himself.

If I truly follow Christ rather than productivity or escapism, I will stop what I'm doing and listen to the Lord through his Word. I will talk to my God. I will sit at his feet even though piles of unfinished things surround me. Sometimes that will look like taking a break to review a Bible verse or pray. But sometimes, when the demands won't stop, it will look like a Spirit-filled heart enjoying his peace in the loud car pool, thanking him for his provision during a run into the grocery store, listening to his prompting in a challenging conversation, and shooting up prayers as I do what's needed to keep life going.

If I truly follow Christ, I will become more like Mary and make choices to bask in the presence of the Savior.

Have you, like Martha, ever sensed God calling you to stop running around and instead give him your attention? How did you respond?

_____

_____

_____

What does your culture or friend group consider to be "the good portion"?

_____

_____

_____

Replace Martha's name with your own in verse 41. How are these words relevant to you right now? Consider spending the next five minutes laying down your burdens and enjoying his presence.

_____

_____

_____

Luke 10:41–42: But the Lord answered her, "Martha, Martha, you are anxious and troubled about many things, but one thing is necessary. Mary has chosen the good portion, which will not be taken away from her."

Let's Be Real

Has there ever been a time that you've regretted spending time with the Lord?

THE ACCOUNT OF MARY AND MARTHA reorders my priorities, but it also leaves me with questions. What in the world did Martha do after this loving rebuke? She still had people in her house and cucumber salad to prep and tables to set. How was she supposed to manage these wide responsibilities and settle herself down to go deep with Jesus? Why is there no verse 43 in Luke 10 to guide us through this quandary?

The absent verse may have told us that Mary jumped up to help later or that others pitched in. Maybe the meal got on the table a few minutes or even an hour late. Maybe Martha realized later with a guilty pang, like I often do, that the panic was unnecessary. Maybe she was grieved and embarrassed by her complaints and accusations and bitterness. Maybe she recognized the effects of the fall inside her. Maybe she asked Jesus to forgive her.

Maybe the verse is missing because obeying Jesus includes trusting him with the results without a guarantee. We don't always know how things will work out practically when we choose the good portion. When we turn from the task, or the grief, or the worry at hand to sit at Jesus's feet (or better yet, bring it with us in prayer) our human nature balks. What will it possibly accomplish?

Instead of giving us a verse 43, God gives us Matthew 6:33. Most likely, Martha had heard reports of the recent sermon Jesus had given on the mountain or even been there herself. Standing before a multitude, he spoke the words that must have left his listeners wondering: "But seek first the kingdom of God and his righteousness, and all these things will be added to you."

If we seek God first, before the list is checked off and all the problems are solved, God will give us "all these things." But will those things get my table set? Will they get Mary off her behind and into this kitchen to help me? Will they bring me the relief I long for?

"These things" that will be given to us, simply put, are exactly what we need for the life God has appointed us (Philippians 4:19). His loving providence is infinitely more attuned to our real needs than our changing desires are anyway. So don't waste your life worrying, but spend it on God, and watch his fatherly hand provide all that he knows is best for his children.

Dr. Martin Lloyd-Jones explains it this way: "Put God, His glory and the coming of His kingdom, and your relationship to Him, your nearness to Him and your holiness in the central position, and you have the pledged word of God Himself through the lips of His Son, that all these other things, as they are necessary for your well-being in this life and world, shall be added unto you."[6]

How radically different would our lives be if we took Jesus at his word, receiving from him the strength, vision, power, and love that he offers for our exact situations? What joy and relief he holds out to us! What hope and courage he shares. How kindly he calls us to come. We are to "seek the kingdom," not to prove our goodness (an impossible task) but because he is so much more satisfying and beautiful than anything or anyone else!

If Martha had wiped her hands on her apron and sat down to listen to Jesus, she wouldn't have regretted it. When we seek God, even when it doesn't make sense or feel productive, we'll never look back and wish we hadn't because we will have received exactly what is best for us. He has promised.

How could Jesus's analogy of the birds in Matthew 6 have helped Martha? How can it help you?

_____

_____

_____

In our passage today, Jesus commands us not to be anxious but instead to seek the kingdom. How can prioritizing God's kingdom over our own counteract anxiety and foster peace in our hearts?

_____

_____

_____

What would it look like for you to "seek first the kingdom of God and his righteousness"? Do you believe he will give you what you need in response?

_____

_____

_____

Matthew 6:33: But seek first the kingdom of God and his righteousness, and all these things will be added to you.

Second Chances

IDENTIFY

In what situations do you hesitate to come to Jesus for a drink, even though you have an open invitation?

IF WE'RE NOT CAREFUL, our rushed hearts can turn the pursuit of the LORD into another item on the task list. But loving God is not a box to self-importantly check off a list; it's answering a call to come home. Our Creator knows exactly how to help us accomplish the wide assignment he's called us to while abiding deep within his love. No mundane job can be drudgery when done in the presence of the living Christ. No busyness can cancel out the peace that comes from heaven.

On the last and greatest day of the Feast of Tabernacles, one of the great celebrations to commemorate God's faithfulness, Jesus stood up and claimed God's words in Isaiah 55 as his own, crying, "If anyone thirsts, let him come to me and drink. Whoever believes in me, as the Scripture has said, 'Out of his heart will flow rivers of living water'" (John 7:37–38). Jesus is the source of all refreshment, a wellspring of life so abundant that it overflows the confines of our own lives and swirls into the barren hearts of others.

There is no perfect way or time to accept this invitation, and we certainly can't wait until there is "time." No special journals or pens or plans are needed. Lofty thoughts or flowing phrases are not required. We just need to come. When we open his Word, he'll speak to us by his Spirit. When we open our mouths in prayer, he'll listen and love. Sometimes we need to step away from the fray and give ourselves wholly to him. Other times we need to commune with him while creating a spreadsheet or wielding a vacuum cleaner. The only thing we can't do—that we're fools if we do—is ignore him. Opt out. Stay in the other room and tell ourselves that fixing the problem or finishing the task on our own will bring greater joy.

Jesus has made coming to him simple. Because he accomplished the formidable work of redemption on the cross, the only move left for Christians is to step into his presence. That is the step that we need to take regardless of how overwhelmed we may feel. Step into the fountain. Come to the waters.

Lies will come: *You don't have time. You're not spiritual enough. It won't help. You've tried this before.* Your sinful nature will flex its muscles: *You can do this yourself. You don't need God. Just keep hustling and complaining.* But the gospel obliterates excuses.

We boldly come as beloved children to a smiling Father because of the willing sacrifice of his beloved Son. God loves and lavishes us with grace through no merit of our own, and he pours out goodness to his children. His truth disintegrates lies. His love forgives sins. His death and resurrection blast through every barrier between needy child and heavenly Father.

Let's not miss the fact that both sisters came to Jesus. One came quietly, immediately making the right decision and enjoying her Lord. Another came sharply, sleeves damp with dishwater, complaining to Jesus about the unfairness of life. But she came. And what did Jesus do? He loved her. He listened to her. He answered her. He adjusted her perspective. He told her the truth that would help her the most. This is what Jesus will do for you and me when we haul our frenzied souls before him, kicking and screaming and swearing that all we really need is a changed situation.

God loves us into transformation. His redemption is deep and wide. Our dear Martha holds the honor of quoting one of the most profound confessions about Christ in the New Testament. This time she was immersed not in busyness, but in the fresh grief of her brother's death. Even in her confusion about Jesus's timing, Martha confessed for the ages: "Yes, Lord; I believe that you are the Christ, the Son of God, who is coming into the world" (John 11:27).

"How did Martha come to this?" R. Kent Hughes asks in his commentary on Luke. "She had chosen the 'one thing.' She sat with Mary at Jesus' feet. She was an avid hearer of the Word. And the church was built on the granite of such confession."[7]

We don't need to remain stuck in our irritation and busyness and complaining. We can run to our Redeemer. Jesus of Nazareth knows you, loves you, and welcomes you—the empty cup—to come to him—the overflowing fountain. Living a deep Christian life and a wide busy life are not mutually exclusive. In Christ, we are called and empowered to do both, and in the process find true joy. Let's not miss the best portion.

How have you seen God "love you into transformation"?

_____

_____

_____

What area of struggle or sin can you bring to your Redeemer, receiving his help and forgiveness? Do you believe he welcomes you in any state?

_____

_____

_____

How does Martha's great declaration of Christ encourage you? What does it say about the way he treats us in our sins?

_____

_____

_____

John 7:37: On the last day of the feast, the great day, Jesus stood up and cried out, "If anyone thirsts, let him come to me and drink."

TAKE AND SHARE

View your busyness and stress not as an excuse to avoid fellowship with God, but as a reason you need him even more. Come to the fountain with your unfinished business trailing behind you, and don't just stand at the edge. Wade in and splash around and be refreshed by our Lord's presence. Then pull your family and friends in to join you, introducing them to the one who delights to refresh their weary souls as well.

WEEK 2

Pray

A King's Crisis

Too often, we assume our situations aren't important enough to bring to God, or worse, we think we don't need his help. We try to control our circumstances by worrying, manipulating, and obsessing, instead of humbly praying and watching what God can do. This week we'll meet a king whose dreams were falling down around him and learn from his prayer to the King of kings.

Puzzle Pieces

IDENTIFY

What walls feel like they are crumbling in your life right now, even though you're trying to hold them up?

JIGSAW PUZZLES ARE QUIRKY THINGS. You spend hard-earned money for a cardboard picture that's cut into hundreds, sometimes thousands, of pieces just so you can put it back together. It seems like a crazy hobby when you think about it, but people seem to love them.

Whether you enjoy puzzles or not, we can all agree there is something satisfying in seeing pieces come together. Scattered grays and blues become waves crashing on a lighthouse. Pinks and yellows become Victorian houses on a sunlit street. The finished picture speaks of meaning and unity and purpose.

Our lives sometimes feel like puzzles scattered at our feet: some pieces under the bed, some lost down the heating vent, and most staring back up at us as fragments of a potential that may never be realized. The box top that reveals the picture? Nowhere to be found. *When is life going to come together?* we wonder.

The jumble looks different for all of us: work, school, marriage, church, friends, future. Family responsibilities. Workout plans. Home projects. And then there are those difficult gray pieces that blend into everything: loneliness, disappointments, strained relationships, wayward kids, body image, comparisons, fear of failure, your expectations for personal growth. Sometimes it even feels like most of the pieces are lost down the vent.

I don't think jigsaw puzzles were around in King Hezekiah's time, but Hezekiah was familiar with a puzzled heart. The kingdom he ruled was crumbling to pieces through the fingers of his outstretched hands.

I'm one of the good ones, Lord, he probably thought as he remembered years spent undoing his father's wrongs. He had demolished pagan altars, pried open the rusty temple doors, and done his best to follow God. *How can this be happening?*

The Assyrians, a world power, had already conquered the surrounding nations, and now they threatened Judah, Hezekiah's home and kingdom. He tried to satisfy them by stripping God's holy temple to nakedness, tearing its gleaming gold from doors and walls and handing it to the enemy. Humiliated, Judah was safe for just a moment before Assyrian leaders were back at the city gate shouting taunts in earshot of the people: "On what do you rest this trust of yours?" (2 Kings 18:19).

How often has that question resounded in believers' minds through the ages, like the toll of an awful bell ringing doom and determinism, darkness and despair? You've probably heard its echoes in your own ears as you lay awake at night, convinced that all your bleak predictions for the future will come true and that God probably won't do much to help.

We may not rule a kingdom, but our lives can still feel like they're crumbling. As hard as we work, we can't seem to prop up all the walls. Something is always falling apart; a relationship or job isn't working out, and our plans just aren't materializing.

Where do we rest our hope when circumstances aren't looking very good? Circumstances like this force us to understand that there is only one stable, unshakable foundation for our lives—our Lord, who is as present and active as ever, who even in the darkness is working his unsearchable will in ways we can't yet see. We rest it in the one who is never overwhelmed, never discouraged, never frustrated, but is perfectly poised to shine his glory through the cracks in the crumbling stones for the joy of his people. God will be true. Hezekiah found that out, and so will you.

So take heart today, whatever your circumstances, because the Lord is at work. Jerry Bridges reminds us that "Nothing can be more consoling to the man of God, than the conviction that the Lord who made the world governs the world; and that every event, great and small, prosperous and adverse, is under the absolute disposal of Him who doth all things well, and who regulates all things for the good of his people." And that includes you.[8]

What puzzle pieces in your life seem like a jumble of things that don't make sense or go together?

_____

_____

_____

If someone asked you "On what do you rest this trust of yours?" (v. 19), what would your honest answer be? If your answer is "God," what does that look like in your life?

_____

_____

_____

What is one way God has been faithful to you in the past year?

_____

_____

_____

Psalm 56:3–4: When I am afraid, I put my trust in you. In God, whose word I praise, in God I trust; I shall not be afraid. What can flesh do to me?

When Nightmares Come in the Mail

IDENTIFY

What do the voices in your head tell you about your future, and where do you go with them?

AS A KID, I LOVED READING *Alexander and the Terrible, Horrible, No Good, Very Bad Day*. Right out of bed he gets gum in his hair, trips over his skateboard, and drops his sweater in the wet sink. Not a good start.

Hezekiah wasn't having a good day either—or year for that matter. His kingdom was being assaulted by Assyrian enemies whose leader, the Rabshakeh, proclaimed disaster to Hezekiah's fearful people, informing them that every allied nation, as well as their own God, would fail them utterly. His words sank like stones into their hearts, but they kept silent. Hezekiah's right-hand man, Eliakim, begged that the threats be made in Aramaic so the people on the wall wouldn't understand and panic, but no mercy was given. "Why shouldn't I speak," the Rabshakeh scoffed in the common language, "to the people 'who are doomed with you to eat their own dung and to drink their own urine?'" (2 Kings 18:27). Why shouldn't they know that their own worst nightmares will come true?

How similar those words are to the voices of worry in our own minds, telling us the worst things we can imagine will surely happen, and we'll be alone when they do.

After the threats came the lure of false promises, the same one that hissed from the serpent in Eden, assuring the people that all would be well if they turned from their naive trust in God to a new and better master, one who would delight their appetites and fulfill their longings. There would be olive trees for one, and honey for another; wine and vineyards for this one, and sprawling lands for that one. If only they would surrender and follow him, the tempter beckoned.

In anguish, Hezekiah "tore his clothes and covered himself with sackcloth and went into the house of the LORD" (2 Kings 19:1).

I'm guessing he ran. Sackcloth and torn clothes symbolized deep emotional pain—desperation. He ran because the words felt true. He ran because he heard his own secret fears shouted by real voices to real ears. He ran because doubt was chasing him like a hungry coyote that would have its prey. Instead of going to his strategists and counselors, he went to the house of God.

I love that the Bible tells us real stories. It doesn't send its words down the Bible factory conveyor belt where all the nasty ones are thrown out and the nice ones are wrapped with shiny foil like little Hershey Kisses in neat rows. The Bible gives us rough stuff—true stuff. It makes us sit up and pay attention and see glimpses of our own lives.

I am consoled to meet a righteous king who is scared witless and maybe even running in panic, tunic flapping, to God. Why? Because it means I'm not the only one. Even the bravest figures of the Bible have trouble standing against fearful circumstances. Even heroes are stung by the darts of doubt and fall to pieces on the floor, not because of the situations themselves, but because of fears churning and rising in their hearts.

Have you ever heard voices predicting that all your worst fears will come true? They can cripple us. Being left out or left behind is a battering ram at the gates of our hearts. Disappointed hopes are flattening. And yet as Christians we are called to more than listening to our own emotional counsel, convincing as it may seem in the moment. Sometimes the best thing to do is run—run straight to God.

God sent Hezekiah an encouraging word in his distress. Isaiah the prophet walked onto the scene and informed him that God would distract Assyria from carrying out its threat (2 Kings 19:6-7). And God did. His enemies backed off, and Hezekiah breathed.

Then he got the mail.

In it was a letter from the king of Assyria that started the spin cycle all over again. The letter told him not to think for one minute that his God would be faithful. Only a fool would believe that. The letter told Hezekiah that God was a deceiver—a fake. The hope that God would help was a vain one; fear and trauma would surely rule his life and bring him to ruin, and that was the end of it. Envelope closed.

Would God be faithful to his promises? Could God be working a master plan of salvation when the whole world was falling apart? Hezekiah remembered what he knew to be true and hung on for dear life. And sometimes that is our assignment. When circumstances discourage us, we exercise faith by remembering who God is and hanging on, waiting for the morning. God will honor such trust and prove himself faithful every time.

The people working on the wall heard voices that predicted dreadful things (vv. 27–35). When are you most vulnerable to hearing similar voices?

_____

_____

_____

When do you feel tempted to believe your faith in God is naive and that following other cultural influences might be better? Are you believing that now?

_____

_____

_____

When a threat surfaces in your life, do you typically run to God? If not, where do you run first? What would running to God look like?

_____

_____

_____

Psalm 130:5–6: I wait for the LORD, my soul waits, and in his word I hope; my soul waits for the Lord more than watchmen for the morning, more than watchmen for the morning.

Spreading It Out

What keeps you from pouring your heart out before the Lord? What small or significant situations could you bring to him today?

L IKE OUR OWN SCATTERED PUZZLES, Hezekiah's life was in pieces. He was supposed to know what to do, but he didn't. He was supposed to be powerful, but his opponent dwarfed him. How had he gotten here? It seemed that just yesterday he was a boy himself, dreaming of a blessed future, but now he wore a crown that mocked him. He saw jagged pieces all over the floor—of reputation and legacy and responsibility, and especially happiness. But after he read every ugly word of the letter from Assyria's king, he again "went up to the house of the LORD and spread it before the LORD."

I love that line. He gathered the pieces of his splintered life and carefully spread them out before the God who had formed him in his mother's womb and called him to rule over this vast nation of humans he had neither power nor wisdom to protect. He laid them before the God who knew.

He spread out the black pieces: the violence of the Assyrian threats, their history of conquest and hatred, and the doom that was coming. The red pieces: his distraught heart and hopeless strategies, his raw bleeding soul. The greens: the blessings God had given, the hopes and dreams he had, the fields of his nation. The blues: the starry heavens that God showed to his ancestor Abraham and that housed the star that shone for him. And then the golds: the crown of the king of heaven and his own tiny version that sat on his bowed head. Hezekiah offered them all to the Lord in prayer.

Years before, God had told Solomon, "If my people who are called by my name humble themselves, and pray and seek my face and turn from their wicked ways, then I will hear from heaven and will forgive their sin and heal their land" (2 Chronicles 7:14). Hezekiah accepted the invitation to humbly come before God in his time of need. We can do this too, except there is no need to run to a physical temple to meet with God; we don't need to go anywhere. Because of Christ, we have the very presence of God living inside of us through his Holy Spirit, who is always available to us.

What message plagues your mind, informing you of the futility of your efforts or the meaninglessness of your days? What pieces of life have you dropped on the floor with no hope of putting them back together? The God in whom all things hold together (Colossians 1:17) invites you to gather up the very things that overwhelm you and lay them out before him, one by one, a show and tell of your soul to the most caring and powerful Teacher who ever lived.

I've followed Hezekiah's example many times. I wish I would run to God immediately like he did when faced with the wreckage of a situation, but I usually stare at it, stew on it, sit in it far too long, hoping that my own mental calisthenics will order my life and fix my heart. It doesn't happen. Finally I go to him, and what a sweet reception I receive.

I've spread out piles of life decisions. I've spilled armloads of sin—impatience, bitterness, judgments—that seemed to rule me despite my best efforts. I've laid out feelings that needed to be sorted and insecurities that needed to be set straight. You can even come carrying pieces of your own heart to spread before him.

Recently, I was figuring out what to wear to a special wedding. One dress hung too long, making me look like a weird Disney princess. The other zipped only if I held my breath, and I figured I'd suffocate before the end of the ceremony. So I took it off, exhaled, and started to complain about my lack of time to shop. Then I remembered Hezekiah. I realized that we can even spread our small problems, our little twenty-piece puzzles, before the Lord. I prayed. "God, here are the pieces of a ridiculously small situation that I can't fit together, but you can. I give them to you and ask you to make a better picture than I can. You know what you're doing Lord. I don't. Put the puzzle together."

What was the significance of Hezekiah spreading the letter before the Lord (v. 14)?

_____

_____

_____

What would it look like for you to spread the various pieces of your life before the Lord, bringing him into the details of your situations?

_____

_____

_____

Do you assume there are situations too small for the Lord to care about? God welcomes us to bring him all our cares. Bring a few of your small cares to him now.

_____

_____

_____

BELIEVE

Psalm 145:18: The LORD is near to all who call on him, to all who call on him in truth.

No Holding Back

In what ways are you forcing pieces of your life puzzle together instead of letting God put them together? Do you believe he has a beautiful picture in mind?

PRAYING DOESN'T ALWAYS FEEL NATURAL. Our inner skeptic tells us it won't do any good and that we've come to God before and it hasn't solved our problems. The voice of doubt instructs us to just jam the puzzle pieces we can find together, even if they don't fit, to make a crude picture. And we'll settle for that picture of our lives, one that our own clumsy fingers have forced together in unbelief and self-sufficiency, a far cry from the well-crafted scene that God is creating with meticulous detail.

Hezekiah came to the Lord quickly, and he came prayerfully. On his knees with his problems spread out around him, he spoke to God. As we come with our own hands full of pieces, let's pray along with his beautiful prayer in 2 Kings 19:14–19. As Hezekiah did, let's acknowledge God's greatness, present our needs honestly, and ask him to do what we can't.

Given the circumstances, we would understand if he threw down his burden immediately, but Hezekiah first acknowledges God's greatness: "O Lord, the God of Israel, enthroned above the cherubim, you are the God, you alone, of all the kingdoms of the earth; you have made heaven and earth." His worship of God reminds him that although it sure does feel like the Assyrians rule the whole world, wielding a hammer that will bludgeon all that is good, that's incorrect. It just feels that way. God rules. God alone. He governs not just some, but all of the kingdoms of the earth—including Judah. Voicing biblical truths quells panic and washes us with the quieting reality of God's sovereign omnipotence.

In our own lives, it sure does feel like the engine of a broken relationship has the power to chug right off the track into the woods and end in wreckage for everyone. It sure does feel like our loneliness and disappointments will rain their drizzle down every single day from now till forever. It sure does feel like our tiny savings, less than everyone else's we know, rules every decision we make and keeps us from all the best things in life.

Not so. These thoughts don't factor in our gracious God, so committed to our bright future that he gave his own Son to ensure it, enfolding us in a story far more glorious than our own. Enthroned above, God rules over every large and small situation on earth for his own glory and the good of his children. So we trust him day by day, year by year, submitting our lives to his loving hands. Hezekiah starts there, and so should we.

Hezekiah then *tells God the problem as honestly as possible*. God can handle the truth. He asks God to "see" and "hear" the words of the terrible letter that threatens his world. He describes the reality of the situation: "Truly, O Lord, the kings of Assyria have laid waste the nations and their lands . . ." No added drama here. It's all called for and then some. This threat is real.

We can tell God how it is. *Lord, this thing is big and really scary. I don't know what to do or which avenue to pursue or how I can keep going like this. I think I'm headed for disaster.* The one who numbers the hairs on our heads can handle the information. More importantly, his mighty love is down on the floor, right beside us in all the mess, eager to comfort and help and heal and lead. The one who willingly laid his bloody back on a jagged cross for us will sit on the floor with us too.

I remember a ridiculous struggle I experienced several years ago that had me by the throat. Simply put, I was discontent with my home in the suburbs. I could tell the struggle a thousand times that it was silly, that I was just a spoiled brat and was more mature than this, but it didn't listen. I must have been on some kind of misguided homesteading kick because my perfect house just hemmed me in. Sin distorts, and my generous lawn became a prison yard, the shrubs at the edge the prison wall. I needed more space. I needed to breathe. I needed orchards and forests and fields for my kids to run in. I looked out my kitchen window and suffocated. Well, not actually, but it felt like it.

Was this a spoiled brat American problem? Absolutely. Was it a young-mom-at-home-a-lot-stepping-on-Legos problem? Yes, certainly. But was it real? Yes! I talked to people, of course subtly to preserve my reputation. I prayed here and there. I read the Bible. But one rare night when I had the house to myself, I spread it all out before God, in gut-honest detail. I named the feelings, the jealousies, and the specific dreams. I explained the stupidity and what I knew to be true. I confessed my own helplessness and the absurdity of my discontent. I acknowledged God's strength and my lack of it. And God met me powerfully. I didn't hear an angelic voice or see a pillar of cloud, but I experienced the unmistakable presence of God convicting me, assuring me, and reordering my heart.

God so often does this when we actually come to him instead of trying to work things out on our own or deciding ahead of time what God will or won't do. He simply loves to meet with his children, and that means that if you're in Christ, he loves to meet with you. What is holding you back?

_____

What does Hezekiah acknowledge about God's greatness? Take a few minutes and acknowledge those things to God.

_____

_____

What needs did Hezekiah present to the Lord? Take a few minutes and honestly present your needs to the Lord.

_____

_____

How does God's sovereign ruling of the details of the world help you trust him for your own smaller needs?

_____

_____

CONSIDER

BELIEVE

2 Kings 19:15b–16: "O LORD, the God of Israel, enthroned above the cherubim, you are the God, you alone, of all the kingdoms of the earth; you have made heaven and earth."

The Damsel in Distress
Meets the Hero

What was a meaningful time of prayer that you still remember? Why was it special?

THE IRONY OF SPENDING TIME IN PRAYER when we're maxed out in life is that though it feels like wasted time, it's the most productive action we can take. Hezekiah made his wisest, most kingly move when he bowed in humility before the King of kings, not accusing and demanding, but trusting and asking.

After acknowledging God's greatness and telling him the problem as honestly as possible, Hezekiah asked God to do what he couldn't. "So now, O Lord our God, save us, please, from his hand, that all the kingdoms of the earth may know that you, O Lord, are God alone." Surrounded by his letter and his fears, Hezekiah came to God in faith that he would bring good to his people and glory to his name. He came to the Savior asking for salvation.

God's fierce Father's heart loves his children. He loves us in the hopeful mornings and in the long nights when we hear the thumps of the battering ram at the gates of our hearts. He calls us to daily, and nightly, entrust our lives to the hands that already hold them.

The act of praying didn't help Hezekiah in his crisis like some kind of meditative mindfulness technique. God who heard his prayer was the hero of the story; the king, in this case, was the proverbial "damsel in distress." God rode in on his steed and slew the enemy. The angel of the Lord literally came in the night and struck down thousands of men in the Assyrian camp. At the sight of the dead bodies and the annihilation of his power, Sennacherib "departed." God sent him back where he came from. You can read about it in the remainder of 2 Kings 19, where God reveals that he's been watching Assyria's evil deeds all along. He's been present and involved the whole time, missing nothing, and now he will defend his very own with a mighty arm. We can be sure that God, in Christ, will slay our enemies as well. He already has.

No catastrophic kingdom-crashing problem that you or I might face compares to the problem of our sin separating us from God. This problem is devastating and eternal, weighty beyond imagining. Nothing compares. But our holy God, watching all along, didn't punish his enemies this time. He punished his beloved Son instead. Jesus willingly laid down his glory and his life to rescue us from eternal death and secure for us eternal life.

Nothing could thwart God's plan that he established from the beginning of time to dazzle all creation with his glory: no enemy attackers, no fears, no losses, no defeats. The Lord whose steadfast love endures forever was fully in control and at work for his people.

This same Father who sent his beloved Son to die for us will do all that is needed to provide the eternal best for his children. Because that eternal best might be beyond what our finite minds can fathom, we may deal with sadness, confusion, and impatience as we wait for it all to come together. But we can be sure that the apostle Paul's rhetorical question in Romans 8:32 is as obvious as he intended it to be: "He who did not spare his own Son but gave him up for us all, how will he not also with him graciously give us all things?" Will he really give us all things? Of course he will!

"All things" are yours. God will answer your prayers with exactly what his sovereign wisdom knows is best for you—nothing more, nothing less. Whether we see his plan come together on this side of eternity or the next, the God who "upholds the universe by the word of his power" (Hebrews 1:3) is at work, creating a picture that only he can produce, the one we'll stand before slack-jawed in the art museum of heaven. The skill of the painter! The detail! The colors! The intricacies! And you can't even see where the pieces come together. It's a masterpiece.

In addition to the protection of his kingdom, what was a reason Hezekiah asked God to act (v. 19)? How can this help our prayers?

_____

_____

_____

What are some ways God has already made a good picture from some challenging pieces of your life?

_____

_____

_____

How can we balance concern for our own smaller kingdom issues and God's eternal kingdom issues?

_____

_____

_____

Romans 8:32: He who did not spare his own Son but gave him up for us all, how will he not also with him graciously give us all things?

TAKE AND SHARE

Bring your complicated self and situation to the Lord in prayer today. Stop trying to fix everything on your own and instead come to him with the pieces, praying through them one by one. Believe, with Christ's blood as a pledge, that the Father who gave his Son for you will care for each one of the details of your life. Entrusting yourself to him will free you to care for others in their own challenges, showing them the heart of Christ who loves and welcomes them as well.

Fight

The Savior's Battle

Identifying the temptations and lies that lurk in our hearts allows us to address them with God's Word and see change. This week we embark on that adventure, guided by Christ himself as we consider his battle with temptation in the wilderness.

Seeing Through the Fog

IDENTIFY

How often do you use summary words like *overwhelmed, stressed,* or *busy* to disguise specific temptations in your life?

FOG IS TO MYSTERY what sunsets are to romance. If you want to add some suspense, some intrigue, some depth to a scene, roll in the fog.

It was the Battle of the Bands in my high school auditorium, and I sat at the grand piano in my best alternative music getup, trying my hardest to be mysterious and relevant as our band played a song that has since fled my memory. The guitars and drums were pretty good, but what I remember most is that our lead singer must have been having an anxiety attack because he sang the whole thing in the wrong key. We kept up appearances though, and just in case our dark and brooding vibe wasn't convincing enough to hide the lameness, we pumped up the fog machine. It hides everything.

Fog is good for ambiance, but if you want to do more than brood, it needs to go. You need clarity, and the same is true in our spiritual lives. Sometimes foggy words and feelings can hide what is really going on in our hearts, keeping us from the hope and help that Jesus offers.

By foggy words and feelings, I mean vague ones like *overwhelmed, stressed, busy, or down.* These words are helpful in conversation when we don't want to unload our emotional dump truck on the friend we run into in the checkout line. But later, when we have time to think, do we settle for those simple descriptors, or do we think through what's truly going on in our hearts? Do we ask questions like the following: What feels overwhelming to me, and should it? Why do I feel down? Is it because of the interaction with my husband earlier today, and does Jesus have anything to say about that? Why do I feel so busy, and has God called me to it or do I need to change my schedule? It's helpful to identify the temptations behind our foggy negative descriptors and feelings.

Our Bible reading today reminds us that God is a God of clarity. He sees through our words and actions and straight into our souls. What is hazy to us is soberingly clear to him, and he's given us his Word to help us discern the thoughts and intentions of our hearts. The stark words *naked* and *exposed* we read today in Hebrews 4:13 can sound intimidating. Sometimes we'd rather stay hidden in the fog than have our hearts laid bare, but the clarifying light that spills from the pages of Scripture is healthy for our souls. And in those same pages, we find Christ, the friend of sinners, tempted as we are but never yielding to sin, always obedient to his Father. The one who was treated so violently deals with us gently, and when we allow our hearts to be exposed before him, we find that he lovingly covers them with his own righteousness.

Just yesterday while alone in the car, I was aware that something was off. Some tiny thing was bothering me, a gnat in the peace of my soul. "Why are you feeling this way?" I asked myself aloud. "What is it?" I've learned that any unidentified feeling that presses down on me even slightly needs to be named. I must reach my hand into that vaporous cloud and pull out the actual stuff that's in there, nasty as it may be. Sure enough, after a few seconds I located it: some quick words spoken about someone else's success that had threatened me and were now lounging in my subconscious, smoking cigarettes. Now I knew what I was dealing with and could address them by their biblical names: envy and pride. I grabbed these two familiar visitors by the collars, and we went to the Savior together.

You may scoff at the idea of a gnat in your soul. You have bees, hornets even, and your nagging situation isn't a few small words, it's a hot mess, an explosion of fears and failures. If you reached into your cloud of "overwhelmed," you'd need to rent a storage unit for the things you'd find in there. I get it. But we need to identify the contents so that we can take them to God.

Sometimes we simply find innocent feelings in the cloud: hurried thoughts from a busy day or sadness from a disappointment. These are natural and human, and after identifying them, we can take them to the Lord in prayer and let them go. Other times we'll pull out contents that are not so innocent. We'll spend the remainder of this week learning how to deal with those temptations. In either case, let's be courageous enough to identify what's in our hearts so that we can bring it to the feet of our merciful Savior.

Are you more aware of "foggy" negative feelings than specific temptations in your heart? List some of them.

_____

_____

_____

Have you ever had something bothering you, like I did in the car, and had to think hard to figure out what it was? Is there something "off" in your life now?

_____

_____

_____

Are you reading the Bible on a regular basis so that God's truth can clarify what's in your heart? If not, how could you increase your Bible intake?

_____

_____

_____

Hebrews 4:12–13: For the word of God is living and active, sharper than any two-edged sword, piercing to the division of soul and of spirit, of joints and of marrow, and discerning the thoughts and intentions of the heart. And no creature is hidden from his sight, but all are *naked* and *exposed* to the eyes of him to whom we must give account (emphasis added).

Jesus Felt

Are there ways you fill your emptiness that you wouldn't want Jesus to see?

J ESUS WAS EMOTIONAL.

You might prickle at that if you're tired of the drama around you. Or you might be emotionally expressive yourself and think, *Of course he was!*

The Bible tells us that Jesus wept at the grave of his friend Lazarus. He showed anger at hypocrisy, compassion for the sick, and joy in obeying his Father. He was amazingly 100 percent human and 100 percent God. I don't know much about being God, but I know a lot about being human, and it has a lot to do with laughter and temptation and hunger and hope. Jesus, the creator of feelings, felt the full range of emotions. In physical ways, his humanity was even rawer than ours because modern comforts like refrigerators and soft mattresses hadn't been invented yet. Jesus lived an earthy life.

Our Savior can sympathize with our weaknesses because he was human like we are. Still, he always brought Scripture to bear on human experience. He didn't skirt around issues with vague terms but instead celebrated specific obedience and condemned specific sins. His honest communication doesn't mean he lacked compassion; on the contrary, he loved people in their struggles and listened well. But God's Word flowed in his veins, and he spoke it with boldness. When the enemy tempted him to give in to his human cravings and compromise obedience, he stood tall and wielded truth.

We can read about the temptation of Christ and picture him strolling about in spiritual rapture for thirty-nine days, and then having a quick conversation with the devil at the end. But the original grammar shows us that he was tempted the whole time and that the three specific incidents we read in the Gospels were the culmination of these difficult weeks.[9]

Jesus's wilderness view was brown, dry, and barren, like our own situations can look sometimes. His body was empty and weak from fasting. He was also looking down the pipeline of a future that promised betrayal, loneliness, suffering, misunderstanding, and ultimately an agonizing death. Even given the joy set before him, it must have felt truly overwhelming. That's when the devil decided to speak, tossing our eternal destiny up and down in the air like a rubber ball. Or so he thought.

Hungry from his forty-day fast, Jesus's body probably craved relief, fullness, and the end of the trial. He'd already fasted a long time, and Satan's temptation to use his power to create bread at this point could have seemed reasonable. Besides being hungry, Jesus was weary. He had lived a perfect childhood, obeying his heavenly Father by not using his divine powers for selfish ends. He never showed off, threw in a humblebrag, or misused his gifts. But now, Satan suggested, might be a great time for him to prove his dominance, beginning his ministry with the bang it deserved. All Jesus had to do was come to his senses and yield to Satan, who seemed to reign at this point anyway. Would it be so bad to take the easier route for once in his life?

In the wilderness, Satan offered everything attractive to Jesus as he suffered: physical satisfaction, vindication and respect from others, and an easy shortcut from the agony of the cross. "All your problems can be solved, Jesus. It's easy. Can't you see I have the answers? Why carry all those burdens? Why suffer?" You can almost see the forked tongue. In each of these temptations, which were certainly more enticing than we can imagine to Jesus in his weakened state, the Savior stood fast, responding with clarity and conviction. He spoke the full and glorious truths of God, revealing Satan's sugarcoated whispers to be the empty lies they always are.

Christ accomplished for us a thousand theological things in his victory in the wilderness, most importantly his continued journey to the cross. But a secondary accomplishment is surely his example of dealing with his temptations head-on, identifying the devil's lies and addressing them with Scripture. Even in his hunger and fatigue, Jesus wielded the sword of the Spirit to fight his battles. Although he felt understandable emotions in response to his trial, he didn't trust those feelings, but instead trusted God. He didn't obey those feelings, but instead obeyed God.

Our own feelings are gifts from God. Although they often guide us rightly, they can also prove to be fertile soil for temptation. Bitterness can grow in the soil of sadness. Self-pity can grow in the soil of fatigue. When we are enticed to mistrust and disobey the most high God because our feelings are telling us to, we need only look to Jesus. Rooted in the eternal love of the Father, our Savior stood the test. He had a job to do, and he fought for us in the wilderness so he could fight for us on the cross.

Jesus's sacrifice on our behalf dashes to bits our doubts about his love for us. Will he be faithful? Will he finish his work? Will he remember us? Will he fight for us? These questions blush in the loving gaze of our Lord Jesus, who stopped at nothing to make us his own. This is the God we are called to trust, the God we have the privilege of trusting regardless of what temptation comes our way. And when we fail, giving into our cravings as we know we sometimes will, he invites us to run again into his presence for forgiveness and grace. We are always welcome.

CONSIDER

Why didn't Jesus create bread to end his fast? Are there ways Satan is tempting you to take an easier route than the one to which God has called you?

_____

_____

In what areas are you tempted to trust and follow your feelings instead of trusting and following God?

_____

_____

How did Jesus fight off temptations in the wilderness to bring you the gospel? Take time to thank him for that right now.

_____

_____

BELIEVE

Matthew 4:4: But he answered, "It is written,
'Man shall not live by bread alone,
   but by every word that comes from the mouth of God.'"

Talking to Temptation

IDENTIFY

Are you good at talking back to your temptations? What do you say?

REMEMBER THAT TIME you took a week off social media and every time you grabbed your phone you felt an almost physical need to scroll through it? It's shocking how powerful a desire can be for a trivial pastime. How much stronger are human longings for actual physical needs?

Consider our Lord, hungry and empty in the wilderness, foreseeing the ridicule and rejection he would experience as he proclaimed the coming kingdom, not to mention knowing what was to come at the end of his earthly ministry. These temptations must have been brutal because they offered him a way out of his future suffering—immediate glory and power instead of torture and death.

Jesus had every "right" to give in to his hunger, his weakness, his cravings. He had every right to be in a funk, too tired to fight. Walking in obedience toward a hard assignment didn't seem to be providing much earthly pleasure at this point. But he didn't give in. He saw straight through Satan's whispers to the lies that lurked there—lies that said relief is better than obedience, a full stomach is better than a clean soul, loving self is better than loving God. He smelled the smoke of hell on the devil's breath. Then he answered those thinly-disguised lies, targeted at his weakness, with the words of his Father. With hunger pains, he said, "Man shall not live by bread alone." In weariness, he said, "You shall not put the Lord your God to the test." In view of an easier road, he said, "You shall worship the Lord your God and him only shall you serve."

Jesus was resolute in a situation more difficult than any we could imagine.

The lesson for us is not that feelings of weakness and fatigue are wrong and we can only talk about them by quoting Bible verses, complete with the reference. That's a quick road to legalistic frustration. The Bible isn't hesitant to show us people in raw lament, fear, and confusion. (It also shows us Jesus enjoying bread.) But it calls us to more.

The first Scripture Jesus quoted reads in full, "Man shall not live by bread alone, but by every word that comes from the mouth of God" (Matthew 4:4). He's saying that we aren't meant to live for immediate satisfaction. There's something far greater. Remember "the better portion" that Jesus told Martha about in Week One? This is it: abiding in God, living according to his ways and his words, and enjoying his presence, which all deliver a soul-satisfying fullness that no steaming loaf of sourdough can touch.

Identifying the temptations that hide in our hearts and the lies that fuel those temptations sounds like a lot of work. The idea of addressing those lies sounds even harder! Isn't it easier to leave them alone, keeping them hidden in the fog of being "overwhelmed" or "worried" or "stressed"? (Then all we have to do is complain, and that's not so hard.) But these habits only hurt us, keeping us from the grace of repentance and change. Jesus is not only willing, but eager, to help us with our burdens (Matthew 11:28). Our struggling hearts are not too much for him, and he can help us live according to his Word, holding every feeling, situation, and temptation up to its clarifying light.

But first we need to be honest about our hearts. Do you feel a general unrest in your soul? Do you find yourself doubting God's good plans for you? Are you tired of exercising patience and trying to love others? Do worries, comparisons, insecurities, and irritations grip you? You are not alone. When you find yourself weary from the nagging temptations of the enemy, it's time for a meeting, an appointment with the LORD of light. I've done this more than once, and waiting until you feel like it never works. None of us want to face the bogeymen that haunt us, but when we bring them to Jesus, he calls them out for the frauds they are.

Tomorrow we'll talk through addressing our temptations step by step, so plan a slightly longer time for that devotion. In the meantime, there is no need to wait. What temptation is harassing you today? Bring it to the Lord in all its ugly detail right now and ask him to help you locate a verse of Scripture that tells you the truth. This will not only encourage you today, but it will serve as good practice for our exercise tomorrow.

Jesus experienced feelings of temptation but did not yield to sin. What does that look like for you?

_____

_____

_____

Are you generally honest about your temptations, or do you try to ignore them?

_____

_____

_____

Have you ever addressed your temptations with specific Scriptures? How did that go?

_____

_____

_____

BELIEVE

Matthew 4:10: Then Jesus said to him, "Be gone, Satan! For it is written, 'You shall worship the Lord your God and him only shall you serve.'"

Believing the Truth

IDENTIFY

What lies have gone unaddressed in your life for years? How would your life change if they were uprooted?

G AME TIME! Grab something to write on and a Bible. Fortunately, you're not in the wilderness sitting on rocks like Jesus was, so settle yourself in a comfortable chair. Now ask the Holy Spirit to help you cut through any spiritual fog that's concealing what's in your heart. We want to find out exactly what's in there.

First, identify what a negative feeling is saying.

Take some time to jot down exactly what you feel about a particular situation as specifically as you can: fears, frustrations, hopes, stresses—get it all out there. He knows it anyway. Instead of writing "Figuring out my future feels hard," write "I'm afraid of making a wrong decision that will ruin the rest of my life. I want to know what I should do in the future and it's hard to trust God with it." It's raw but honest. Instead of "I feel depressed," write "I feel overlooked by God and others," or "I feel like a failure because my grown children aren't doing well." Maybe you're having marriage or friendship troubles and your assessment is "Loving people isn't worth the pain." These words are as honest as hunger, and God wants to feed you.

Second, identify any lies.

Reread what you wrote, and consider whether any lies are present. It may be that your feelings are simply genuine emotions that fit your circumstance, and the best response is to cry or share with a friend, or simply process those feelings before the Lord. But look closely. Even when we're experiencing real hurt and appropriate sadness, lies can attach themselves to pain like invisible parasites, ensuring our spiritual malnourishment. As I've reached into my own cloud over the years, here are some of the lies I've encountered: *I'm alone. God is tired of me and my sin. I deserve an easy and convenient life. God won't be faithful to the people I love so I need to worry about them.* How do I know they're lies? Because the Bible states the opposite. Finding out just what the Bible does say is our next job.

Finally, fight the lie with truth.

Jesus countered Satan's attacks with the same Scriptures that we have access to in our own Bibles. Are we familiar with the weapons of our warfare? We need to equip ourselves with truth to combat the lies that saunter into our minds sounding so convincing. Study passages of God's Word. What did the words mean to the original hearers? What do they say about God? What do they say about us? Write the truths you find next to the lies you listed. Now you can contrast in black and white what your misguided or even sinful feelings say with what your Redeemer says. Ask God to help you live by these truths. My list might look like this:

- *I'm alone:* "It is the LORD who goes before you. He will be with you; he will not leave you or forsake you. Do not fear or be dismayed" (Deuteronomy 31:8).
- *God is tired of me and my sin:* "For you, O Lord, are good and forgiving, abounding in steadfast love to all who call upon you" (Psalm 86:5).
- *I deserve an easier life:* "And he said to all, 'If anyone would come after me, let him deny himself and take up his cross daily and follow me'" (Luke 9:23).
- *God won't be faithful to my loved ones so I need to worry about them.* There are two lies present here (God isn't faithful and worry is helpful) that the following verses address:

   "Your faithfulness endures to all generations: you have established the earth, and it stands fast" (Psalm 119:90).

   "Do not be anxious about anything, but in everything by prayer and supplication with thanksgiving let your requests be made known to God. And the peace of God, which surpasses all understanding, will guard your hearts and your minds in Christ Jesus" (Philippians 4:6–7).

If you are new to the Bible and aren't sure where to begin with a list like this, study tools like concordances and trusted websites are a great help, but consider talking to your pastor as well. We need to wield the Word of God accurately, being careful that we use specific verses as they were intended, not making them say what we want them to say. Your pastor will likely be delighted to help you understand and use the book he loves.

The familiar voices of our temptations won't fade without a fight. Jesus answered his tempter with specific Scriptures. He didn't just remember them or think about them or acknowledge that God may have said something somewhere about that. He directly countered lies with God's Word. If Jesus needed it to fight his battles, I think we might too.

CONSIDER

How did today's exercise help you to identify any lies you've been believing?

_____

_____

_____

What is the best way you can keep the Scriptures that address these lies before you each day?

_____

_____

_____

If you feel ill-equipped to locate biblical truths that apply to your life, what are some tools you can use or people you can ask for help?

_____

_____

_____

BELIEVE

2 Timothy 3:16–17: All Scripture is breathed out by God and profitable for teaching, for reproof, for correction, and for training in righteousness, that the man of God may be competent, equipped for every good work.

A New Soundtrack

IDENTIFY

What is the difference between viewing Jesus primarily as an example or primarily as a Savior?

WHAT IS YOUR MORNING ROUTINE? Make the bed, brush your teeth, do devotions, and exercise? Or fall out of bed on the eighth snooze, crawl down the stairs, and collapse on the couch? In either case, consider starting each morning by reviewing the biblical truths you listed yesterday, asking the Holy Spirit to help you believe and live them. We can pray the words of today's Bible reading, asking that we would "not be conformed to this world, but be transformed by the renewal of your mind" (Romans 12:2). Nothing less than transformation is the goal in these verses, and God's truth can handle the challenge.

If negative feelings circle your heart like vultures, continue to work to identify the lies that are attached to these feelings. Then fight those lies with the weapons you've readied, the specific Scriptures you listed. Read them aloud. Your soul may be surprised to hear its own vocal cords proclaiming these facts, but it will sit up and listen. I've been known to prop a laminated list of truths on my kitchen windowsill. It's like hiding a baseball bat under the bed just in case an intruder comes in—I have a ready defense at hand.

Change is rarely instantaneous. You will likely encounter the same lies trying to inform and tempt and discourage you. But as you meditate on God's truth, making it the soundtrack of your mind, the familiar lies will lose much of their power. The prominence they enjoyed making proclamations over your life will decrease. God's authoritative voice through his Word, so full of grace and truth, will fill your mind and usher out those lies. So keep God's Word before you, meditating on it day and night (Joshua 1:8). For now, we read divinely inspired words on the pages of our Bibles, but the day is coming when we will hear God's voice speak those very words audibly to our own ears.

Sometimes our troubled feelings and temptations and the lies intertwined in them are so deeply rooted that nothing we do seems to move them. Maybe you've memorized verses on grace, but you stagger under a heavy yoke of perceived condemnation. Or you study passages on God's faithfulness, but worry clings to you like a wet coat. These struggles are common, and we aren't equipped to tackle them alone. It's one reason God gave us the church, fellow believers who help us overcome the battles, encouraging us with their presence, reminding us of truth, and helping us see things we can't see—whether it be hidden sin or beautiful ways God is at work in us.

He gave us pastors and counselors who can help us unravel the complexities of certain situations and apply God's truth. It's not weak to admit we need help—the Bible says we are all members of the same body (Romans 12:15) and that God gives grace to the humble (James 4:6). After receiving that aid, we can turn and love others in our lives who are struggling in similar ways, sharing with them what we've learned and showing them how to apply the Word to their own situations. But no matter who is helping whom, the unwavering truth of God's Word should be the primary weapon in the fight.

Our Lord is infinitely more than a helpful example of how to address temptations. As we've seen this week, he battled hunger and thirst and humiliation and terror to purchase our souls from the eternal death we deserve. He fought with tears and prayers and Scriptures and sleepless nights to win us for himself. Unlike the Israelites who wandered for forty years in the wilderness for their sin, Jesus chose righteousness for forty days in the wilderness. He labored on, all the way to the cross, where he exchanged his sinless life for our stained one, loving us to his last breath. Three days later he stepped out of the tomb, victorious. That step meant there is nothing left to fear, only love to enjoy. We can step out into the light as well. The sun feels good

What time of day would be most strategic for you to daily review specific truths that address lies you will probably encounter?

_____

_____

_____

How has this week's study equipped you to deal with feeling overwhelmed?

_____

_____

_____

Would meeting with a pastor or trusted leader assist you in locating Scriptures that could help you? Set up a meeting.

_____

_____

_____

BELIEVE

Romans 12:2: Do not be conformed to this world, but be transformed by the renewal of your mind, that by testing you may discern what is the will of God, what is good and acceptable and perfect.

TAKE AND SHARE

It's time to stop hiding. Ask the Holy Spirit to help you identify any lies that are shaping your life. Replace them with God's life-giving words, and begin living in the good of his promises. Besides speaking those living and active words to yourself, consider specific ways you can share the truths you're learning with others who need them.

WEEK 4

Yield

A Soul's Striving

Are we pushing hard in life for God's glory or for our own? The goal of our striving matters, and God loves us enough to clarify our motives. This week we will fly over the storied life of Jacob, watching God patiently teach a stubborn soul a lesson of love.

Gotta Hustle

IDENTIFY

Is our nonstop hustle and bustle primarily Christ-focused or self-focused?

WE ALL KNOW what our lives "should" look like when we reach certain birthdays. Social media tells us. Our friends' lives tell us. Our own master life plan that we and our stuffed animals agreed on under the covers of our childhood beds tells us: Educated by this age. Boyfriend by this age. Dream job, or romantic husband, or great friends, or toned body, or upscale apartment, or accomplished kids, or spacious home by this age. Love and happiness are assumed; delays and struggles are not.

Dreaming is essential. How would the Wright brothers have endured the failed attempts and crash landings if they hadn't been fueled by the dream of flight? Would Rosa Parks have had the courage to stand—or sit in her case—against racism without a vision of a better life? Dreams inspire us to change the world, but they also become tormentors, swooping down with cold urgency and driving us to fulfill them at all costs, lest we be labeled the failures we fear we are.

In our individualistic culture, the world would have us believe our destiny sits squarely on our shoulders. Book jackets explain *How to Get What You Want* (astoundingly, in thirty days). We sip coffee from mugs that read "Gotta Hustle if You Want That Muscle." Even pillows to cushion our heads instruct us with cruel irony to "Wake Up and Be Awesome," stamping expectations on the dawn of each new day.

Trying to heed the advice, we work out, work hard, work smart. We self-care, self-help, self-brand. We stay strong, stay motivated, stay hydrated. If we tick off all the boxes of our habit trackers, just maybe we can lasso that wild destiny of ours and tame it into obedience.

Jacob, son of Isaac, grandson of Abraham, was busy doing just that. A fighter from the womb, he was an expert at manipulating circumstances to make his own big dreams come true. He finagled the birthright from his twin brother, Esau, symbolizing the future leadership and authority in the family, then further infuriated Esau by impersonating him so he could steal his blessing as well. Which he did. Score.

Jacob wasn't stupid; he knew God was powerful. But he wanted to harness that power for his own benefit, as if God were a great blue genie requiring a few rubs of the lamp. In our day, Jacob might have said he was simply following his dreams.

We may not be stealing birthrights or blessings, but can we see parts of ourselves in this future patriarch? Is our nonstop hustle and bustle primarily Christ-focused or self-focused? Does the pressure we feel overflow from the God of all peace or our attempts to control situations and the people in them to get what we want?

I'm a woman of action. If there is something I can do to make things how I think they should be, I'll do it. And though action can please God, the Kingdom of Trish always beckons. It's comfy there, and everyone loves me. My personal kingdom does require some upkeep: *Friend, I'm sorry I had to slander you to bolster my position in my kingdom. Kids, I'm sorry I had to yell at you to keep my palace perfect. Husband, I'm sorry I had to manipulate you to accomplish my will. Everyone, I'm sorry that the stress of building my kingdom makes me use you instead of love you, but it's a lot of work being god, and I know you understand . . .*

Are we sitting in a knock-off version of the director's chair, like Jacob was, telling people and situations to go this way and that way to ensure that our life movie is made to our liking? Let's not kid ourselves and inflate our own importance. The real director is on the set, and he won't settle for anyone usurping his role.

Jesus suffered and died to forgive our sins of pride and selfish ambition. His unmerited grace provided a second chance to Jacob and to us. No matter how much remaining sin we struggle with, Christ is in us, promising to transform us "into his image with ever-increasing glory, which comes from the Lord, who is the Spirit" (2 Corinthians 3:18 NIV). If we desire to put to death our controlling natures and submit to God's gracious one, we should glance at Jacob but gaze at Jesus.

That means looking our sin in the face, seeing its rampant selfishness and blatant narcissism, and then turning our eyes upon the Savior, taking in the rightness of everything about him. Notice the love in his words, the care in his actions, the joy in his obedience, the sacrifice in his death, the glory in his resurrection. God welcomes us to live in the gaze of the risen Christ, seen and seeing, ever changed by that intimate communion.

What life plan or mental timeline have you made that tells you what should be happening when? What is or isn't on track?

_____

_____

_____

Are there ways you see yourself in Jacob? Do you feel stressed by your own ambitions? How can you tell the difference between your goals and God's?

_____

_____

_____

Ask God to forgive you for trying to manipulate circumstances instead of asking him for help. He loves to forgive us, help us, and lead us rightly.

_____

_____

_____

BELIEVE

2 Corinthians 5:14–15: For the love of Christ controls us, because we have concluded this: that one has died for all, therefore all have died; and he died for all, that those who live might no longer live for themselves but for him who for their sake died and was raised.

Ladders

IDENTIFY

Which do you feel you need most: relationship counseling, life coaching, financial planning, or an encounter with the living God?

N **OBODY THINKS IT'S ODD** that gravity pins us to the surface of the earth because it's all we've ever known. We move laterally, but not up. That's off limits. Our bodies aren't made to go that way; thus, the invention of ladders. The earliest record we have of a ladder reveals that it was made of grass and used to reach a wild honey bee nest.[10] I envision Pooh Bear balancing on it with his honeypot, but historians may not appreciate that.

The tallest ladder I've ever climbed was attached to a silo on my friend's dairy farm. It was straight up, dangerous, and dizzyingly high, but we were barefoot kids who hadn't spent a lot of time pondering mortality. Even so, one look down sent a rush of adrenaline screaming through our nine-year-old nervous systems. The view from the tiny platform at the top was worth every death-defying step though because we just wanted to be "up there."

Everybody does. The Babylonians built their infamous Tower of Babel (to the dismay of every high school student required to learn a foreign language), the Egyptians built pyramids, and the Aztecs even built a gruesome tower made of human skulls. The majority of these ancient ladders were religious in nature. Intuitively, we want to rise from our earthbound station and reach the heavens.

Yesterday we considered Jacob's selfish dreams. Now in today's reading God provides the dream, and its focus is what so many have tried and failed to build: a ladder connecting earth to heaven. The Lord stood above it, declaring that the promises he gave to Abraham would indeed be fulfilled through Jacob. And those promises connected man to God, like a ladder God had built.

Why would Holy God appear to impure man, spanning the distance with a ladder? Why would he stand at the top, speaking rich promises to an earthbound guy who sought only his own glory? Had Jacob's scheming and scamming somehow manipulated God into supporting his plans?

On the contrary, through the dream God shows Jacob, and us, that God's sovereign will is the active force in our lives. Our sense of control is a good game of make-believe. God's initiative accomplishes what lasts without the aid of our conniving. In love, God had decided to bless his people through the ages, declaring that even sinful Jacob would be part of that. Jaw-dropping, pride-exploding grace is what Jacob received from God on High, and it's what we receive as well.

The next morning, Jacob was humble. Mostly. He worshipped God and marked the holy site with a stone, but even after his intimate time with the Lord, his earthy side pulsed and flexed. He just had to get back in that director's chair. The man who fast-talked Esau out of his birthright tried to make a deal with God. "Hey God, if you bless me in these ways, then I'll do some things for you."[11] If we were watching Jacob in a movie, we'd cringe. He still doesn't get it.

The Bible commends hard work, and trusting God doesn't mean sitting around waiting for him to do something. Plans and productivity and perspiration are necessary. The martyrs didn't die in their recliners. But God calls Christians to work enthusiastically for a better glory than their own, a glory he shares with us in lavish generosity.

Sometimes the scurrying and managing that fill our moments are activities assigned by God and he gives us grace to thrive in the chaos. Other times, the chaos is self-inflicted. We commit to more activities than we should to please people and manage our reputations. Trusting our own efforts, we control this, reframe that, and jostle people and plans until they line up to serve our purposes, out of breath from trying to master our destinies.

Thank goodness our kind God rules and reigns in righteousness and wisdom, inviting us to lay down our scribbled schemes and yield to his better will. Although it can feel scary to loosen our grip on our plans and open our hands to him, this is the very posture we were created for—the posture of worship. *Make me who you want me to be, Lord. Take me where you want me to go. Replace my will with yours. Help me love the things you love.*

More than relationship counseling, life coaching, and financial planning, we need encounters with the living God, milestones that mark us and humble us and change us from the inside out. We are welcomed into his presence, where we lift our hearts to him and he pours his grace on us. Are we seeking these experiences with the God who promises to be found by us (Jeremiah 29:13)? Even more than his provisions and gifts, God himself is what we need.

What does God's initiative in the dream show us about him?

_____

_____

_____

Is there a time in your life when you had a significant encounter or revelation of God, seeing him in a new way?

_____

_____

_____

Are there ways you are bargaining with God rather than trusting and obeying him? What is God saying to you about that through this Scripture?

_____

_____

_____

BELIEVE

Ephesians 2:4–7: But God, being rich in mercy, because of the great love with which he loved us, even when we were dead in our trespasses, made us alive together with Christ—by grace you have been saved—and raised us up with him and seated us with him in the heavenly places in Christ Jesus, so that in the coming ages he might show the immeasurable riches of his grace in kindness toward us in Christ Jesus.

DAY **3**

Two Races

IDENTIFY

Do you live life feeling like you're never doing enough?

AN **ARTICLE** in *The Washington Post* tells the story of a middle-aged runner who was spotted in a T-shirt that said, "You haven't run a really good marathon unless you drop dead at the finish line." A week later, while running a marathon, he had a massive heart attack and died.[12] It's a sad, but true, story that makes me want to reconsider all my T-shirt slogans.

This poor man ran hard in a race that taxed his body into heart failure. In a similar way, do we bring on any of our own fatigue? Are we striving ourselves to death—and for what? If you're unsure, consider these questions:

- Do you feel like you're never doing enough and need to go harder?
- Do you tend to control people, correcting and adjusting them to meet your expectations?
- Do you become moody when you don't get what you want and impatient when people slow you down?
- Do you often complain when situations don't meet your expectations?
- Do you have big plans for yourself?
- Do you live frustrated that life doesn't cooperate with you?

If you answer yes to many of these questions, as I do, you may be out of breath from showcasing your own speed rather than running after Christ. Christ paced himself to love others along the way, stopping for the weak and cheering for others' victories. When we race for ourselves, we can be so intent on our own goals that we run people and priorities over, our tread prints on their backs as we dash by.

College students, is love for Christ more important to you than perfect grades and popularity? Moms, do you train your children for godliness or to make them symbols of your own success? Employees, do you work extra hours to highlight Christ's name or your own? Wives, are you busier encouraging your husband or wearing him down so he does life your way? Friend, are you loving your neighbor or burning yourself out trying to be her savior? God's track may pass through rough terrain, but it's a peaceful run, not a stressed-out, selfish dash.

In today's Bible reading, Jacob's race toward prosperity is blocked by his uncle. The manipulator is manipulated, the cheater cheated. How often God uses the disappointment of a blocked path to slow us down and get our attention. Jacob is stuck waiting fourteen years for the wife he desires, and God is working on him in the wait, crumbling his self-sufficiency and pride so Jacob can see beyond himself.

Striving isn't limited to the physical plane; it squirms into the spiritual one too, convincing us we must earn grace through effort and accomplishments. Its Christian name is legalism. Instead of serving, studying, and working in gratitude to our Savior, we do it to boost our worth in God's sight, a laughable endeavor for a God who gave his very life for ours, accomplishing what we could never do on our own.

On Laban's land, Jacob stalled. He wasn't as able as he had thought he was. Fourteen laborious years of waiting for his uncle's approval helped him to see that he was also dependent on God's approval, but that one couldn't be earned. Fourteen years or fourteen million years couldn't buy God's blessing. Jesus took our sin and gave us his righteous life so that we would be acceptable to God. He did what we could never do so our striving can become singing. The work is done.

Which questions at the beginning of today's devotion were yes for you? In what ways do you see self-sufficient striving in your life?

_____

_____

_____

What disappointments or delays are teaching you to wait on God?

_____

_____

_____

Are you striving or singing your way through life?

_____

_____

_____

BELIEVE

Ephesians 2:8–10: For by grace you have been saved through faith. And this is not your own doing; it is the gift of God, not a result of works, so that no one may boast. For we are his workmanship, created in Christ Jesus for good works, which God prepared beforehand, that we should walk in them.

DAY 4

The Wrestling Mat

IDENTIFY

What issues, questions, or sins in your life do you tend to "hide" from God?

HAVE YOU EVER WRONGED A SIBLING and had to face up to it? Maybe you dented their car or stained borrowed clothes. It's a miserable process to go tell them, even if it's just a walk down the hall. Imagine stealing from your sibling in a way that ruined their life, then running away for twenty years and finally coming back to face them. That's a long walk, and it's the one Jacob is taking in our reading today. Even though angels appear to him on the way, he fears that Esau will mow down his entire flock and family in vengeance. Rightly petrified, he makes plans, as always, but he's slowly learning to depend on God, even praying for the first time in this whole long story. And on one dark night on his long, lonely walk back to Canaan, God meets our man, remarkably, in a wrestling match.

I attended a few wrestling matches in high school and hated them. The uniforms were weird and the wrestlers got themselves into the most embarrassing positions, but what I most disliked was the personal tension. Watching two bodies locked in combat, bracing and straining against each other with muscles taut was all too personal for me. Victory and defeat felt epic and devastating, so I left mid-match and found solace in a soft pretzel at the concession stand.

The God who pursues us all in personal ways came to Jacob on the mat, and Jacob engaged. They wrestled all night, tense and personal, sweat-soaked and gritty, mixing breath and blood. Finally, Jacob's opponent, a "man" who later reveals himself to be God in bodily form, injured him, but Jacob wouldn't let go without a blessing. Conquered, Jacob finally longed for God's true blessing instead of his own raggedy ones, and he received it. He was given a new name and a new identity, one that belonged to God.

God is real. He is personal. True interaction with him can be intense, emotional, and a little too honest for our liking. The one whose voice melts the earth is no pushover (Psalm 46:6). Although Christ invites us to boldly come before the throne of grace, as C. S. Lewis so famously wrote in *The Chronicles of Narnia*, "He is not a tame lion."[13]

At times, it can feel easier to talk about God rather than to him, to wrestle with theology rather than with God himself. But you can't pretend too long with our tenacious God. He is too true, too alive to stand aside and watch the charade. Incarnate God came from heaven onto earth's stage, even onto the wrestling mat, to save us and call us and know us and love us. And he has more for us than the mantra on our mug or throw pillow can provide. He will not destroy our dreams but reforge them into something worthy of heaven until they glow with his glory.

Have you engaged God on the wrestling mat? Or have you stood by the side, repelled by such honest dealings and uncivilized behavior? It may be time to step in, bringing with you the ambitions that drive you and facades that hide you, hauling your doubts and fears onto the mat along with the sins so strong they want to define you. Jesus initiated every interaction with us at the cross. He welcomes us in, but he demands honest dealings and open hearts. That is his way. If a dirty, sweaty, tear-stained, honest, even painful interaction with our Lord ensues, he is up for it and will be honest in return. And you will leave with a blessing.

If it's been a long time, you may forget how to honestly engage God or wonder if you've ever done it in the first place. His door is open. Come talk with him, undistracted, unrushed, and unhindered. Put him first in that hour or time you've allotted. Throw your phone out the door if you need to. Tell the Lord, preferably aloud, your real questions, your darkest doubts, your hopes and circumstances and joys. Share what feels overwhelming or discouraging. Confess the sins you're ashamed to admit. You don't have to conjure up any particular emotions; he will bring them if he chooses. Open your Bible to Psalms or other scriptures that are meaningful to you, and beg God to speak to you through them because you are desperate for him. Ask him to convict you, lead you, change you, speak to you, awe you, use you, take you apart and put you back together, do whatever he wants to do in your life. Tell him all you want is him, and if you don't feel that way, ask him to help you feel that way. He loves to answer those vulnerable prayers.

God is too great to play with and too loving to avoid. Our brazen hearts, bent on their own foolish dreams, must yield—in pain, then pleasure—to his vast and wonderful will. Any limp we carry in pursuit of knowing him will be a treasured reminder of his powerful love.

What does the passage we read show about God's initiative toward us and willingness to engage?

_____

_____

_____

Does this passage's description of God wrestling with Jacob surprise you? Why?

_____

_____

_____

What things does God want you to wrestle out with him? What are you waiting for?

_____

_____

_____

BELIEVE

Psalm 62:7–8: On God rests my salvation and my glory; my mighty rock, my refuge is God. Trust in him at all times, O people; pour out your heart before him; God is a refuge for us.

A New Name

IDENTIFY

When have you engaged God deeply about an issue or situation, praying honestly and searching his Word? What was the result?

IF YOU WATCH A HALLMARK MOVIE, you're guaranteed a happy ending. Granted, it will not be subtle. It may include a girl impossibly tripping into a handsome man's arms while decorating a Christmas tree as cotton balls fall from the sky, but hey, at least they're happy. Sometimes we want to see all the loose ends tied up, even if it's a little cheesy and we know it's not real.

Today's Scripture reading delivers a true happy ending in the saga of Jacob and Esau. We find Jacob alive (Esau met him with mercy), renamed, and blessed even more profoundly by God. The change in Jacob's name confirmed God's work in his life. The name Jacob meant deceiver, but Israel meant "strives with God."[14] The first describes a man intent on his own plans; the second a man interacting with the Lord.

The narrative stays real though. Throughout his life we see Jacob pleasing God in one situation and regressing to his selfish ways in the next, confirming what we know: even those who follow the Lord are still works-in-progress who daily need his transforming mercy. We all, even famous Old Testament patriarchs, need a Savior. God in his kindness continues to remake Jacob through visions, lessons, and personal encounters, and he reiterates his blessing. Like a child with a security blanket, Jacob often held tight to his plans and strategies. He felt safe and in control with them. When he slowly opened his hands, God placed in them blessings of eternal value. God had made him a strategist for greater purposes than selfish ambition, and now Jacob could become what he was made to be.

Yielding to God doesn't lessen work. Instead, yielding gives work meaning and motivation. We do what we do to please the Lord. Yielding ultimately brings rest because we aren't trying to play God and hold the world together. We know that he will accomplish his will. Yielding helps us say no to things that aren't priorities because we are no longer proving ourselves by climbing the success ladder, rung by rung, or trying to make everyone love and worship us to achieve our ends. God has provided a different ladder, descended it, and is with us always. Yielding brings blessing.

In a culture that urges us to do whatever is needed to make our own dreams come true, yielding is scary. Our knuckles are white from grasping what we feel will deliver happiness. If we let go of that relationship, career path, body image, or dream, what will become of us? If we don't fight for ourselves and our future, who will fight for us?

The God who enters the wrestling match with us will enter it for us. As Moses told the people when they feared the Egyptians, "The LORD will fight for you, and you have only to be silent" (Exodus 14:14). Is there any greater proof that God loves us and wants the best for us than a bloody cross and a vacant grave?

God didn't breathe into Jacob's sails and move him along in his own personal journey of self-discovery. He didn't empower Jacob with strength to fulfill his fantasies of prestige. God wasn't the wind beneath Jacob's wings. No, he wrestled him to the ground to show Jacob who he was: not an idea, not an energy, not a genie, but God, as real as a weighty hand pinning you down.

God is the director of this spinning earth and our days upon it, and our happy job is to submit to his designs. We can't let the world's clamoring voices confuse us. We are to follow him. In the greatest turn of events in history, God the Son gave up his glory to save us so we could in turn give glory back to him. It's a lot to take in. Jacob finally got it when God conquered him in order to establish him in a role far greater than any he could have imagined, being a conduit of the blessing of God to others. We are called to do the same, freely sharing the love that has been freely shared with us.

As we sacrifice our own selfish ambitions to God, quieting ourselves under his hand and yielding to his will, he will establish us in the very position he created us to hold, its worldly rank meaningless in light of the glorious purpose of God.

What cultural voices most influence your goals? Are they ones you should be listening to?

_____

_____

_____

In what way do we need to be "conquered" in order to serve God rightly?

_____

_____

_____

Are there any areas of your life that aren't fully yielded to God? What would yielding look like?

_____

_____

_____

Genesis 35:3: "Then let us arise and go up to Bethel, so that I may make there an altar to the God who answers me in the day of my distress and has been with me wherever I have gone."

TAKE AND SHARE

Our own master plans will never fulfill us but will drive us until we've ruined whatever stands in our way. Wrestle with God to understand the ultimate rest of knowing Jesus has accomplished for us all that truly matters, and yield to his better way. Then run your new race by slowing down to love others, looking beyond yourself, trusting God's ways, and coming alongside your fellow runners with news of the rest that they too desperately need.

Obey

A Widow's Choice

When we feel depleted, obedience is often the last thing on our minds. But in our quest to have our needs met, are we missing the path of greatest provision? A widow living in Baal country will show us. Her story reveals much about our trustworthy God and the blessing of obedience.

Stuck

IDENTIFY

How would you describe the chapter of life you're living right now? Long? Short? Exciting? Mundane? Exhausting?

DEATH INTRIGUES ME. Not in an eerie kind of way. I'm sensible enough to be sobered by it and grieve the brokenness it leaves in its wake. But as the door swings back and forth between this world and the next, its significance is monumental. I've done a bit of reading about the last days of some of the world's best thinkers, and in an unexpected way, it has kindled my gratitude for the work of Christ on my behalf. The door looks very different when you know the One opening it.

In an earthly sense, death moves a person in a flash from a particular point on the time line of life to the whole line. When an elderly man dies, he stops being viewed as a stooped grandfather with a cane and is remembered as the daredevil teenager, the brilliant chess player, the faithful family man. We enjoy all those seasons of his life at once and do a lot of talking and laughing and crying about him at his funeral lunch over turkey sandwiches and potato chips. Ironically, we're never allowed this view of our own lives, at least on this planet. We always live in the moment, the itty-bitty right now. We can't push or peek any further in life than this moment, try as we might, until dawn glides in tomorrow.

As you read this page, you are living in a chapter of a life God is writing. You don't know what chapter it is, how long it will be, if it will be a cliff-hanger to some momentous news or a description of faithful monotony. It's been years since I read *Farmer Boy* by Laura Ingalls Wilder, but I think there were entire pages dedicated to the spreads of food that Almanzo's mother prepared for dinner. She must have cooked her way through the chapters of her life.

You might be in the middle of an overwhelming chapter in your life story. Maybe it's a long chapter. Maybe it feels like the only chapter, like Bill Murray in *Groundhog Day*, where he does the same thing over and over and over. And over. Try as you might to jump up and out of the pages to read the next section or at least see when it's coming, you're stuck down there in the 12-point font. This moment is a word in a sentence. God has designed it that way, and his chiseled hands are purposefully scripting each sentence of your story, enfolding it mysteriously into his own.

The hands that script those words are the same ones that formed the intricate systems of your body, as we read today in Psalm 139. They knitted and wove you together with skillful precision, readying you for the life in which you could best glorify God. You may feel "stuck" in your current situation, but the God who made you "fearfully and wonderfully" knows exactly what he's doing. The hands that formed you will also sustain and guide you through each day already written in his book.

How does today's Scripture reading affect you? If God has written all the days of your life in his book even before one of them occurred, how should that change the way you live?

_____

_____

_____

What opportunities does this chapter of your life offer that you could take better advantage of?

_____

_____

_____

Tell God where you feel "stuck." Ask him for greater faith for where he's placed you.

_____

_____

_____

Psalm 139:16: Your eyes saw my unformed substance; in your book were written, every one of them, the days that were formed for me, when as yet there was none of them.

Gathering Sticks

IDENTIFY

In what area of life does obedience feel tiresome, unnecessary, or not worth the bother?

_____

THE WIDOW OF ZAREPHATH'S CHAPTER was a difficult one. She didn't even have a name, at least one that anyone bothered remembering. She's just called "the widow" by the writer of 1 Kings. A quick bio on her reads: Widowed mother of one son. Living in a small town outside Israel in the ninth century BC. Surviving in abject poverty during a drought. Likely to die of starvation.

The poet Emily Dickinson asks,

I'm nobody! Who are you?

Are you - Nobody - too?[15]

The widow of Zarephath would have answered a definite yes. But in one of the many surprises of Scripture, God highlights this little character in a particularly dark chapter of her life, one she thought would be her last. This woman was not overwhelmed by toothpaste choices or disorganized email but by sheer survival. She'd given it her best go, trying this and trying that, but ultimately she'd failed. The drought swooped down on her poverty like a seagull and stole the last crumbs. Starvation moved from worry to terror to reality, and as a widow, she shouldered the burden alone, wondering how she could bear to watch her son die. Maybe she'd go first.

At the same time, God was busy writing the pages of Elijah the Prophet's story, telling him to go find this very widow to—of all things—ask for food. Up till now, God had miraculously fed Elijah by ordaining ravens to bring him "bread and meat in the morning, and bread and meat in the evening" (1 Kings 17:6). Birds literally delivered his dinner. But God stopped the aviary Doordash and now sent him to the most unlikely of hostesses, a single mom dying of starvation in Nowhereville. God does the strangest things.

Elijah finds her while she's gathering kindling for her and her son's last meal, and he asks for dinner. I can't begin to imagine her feelings at this moment. The stress. The grief. The dark irony.

Maybe you're not gathering sticks for your last meal, but the sticks you are gathering, the tasks that fill your hours and days, hold no happy purpose. You have no smile. From what you can see, the horizon is a vast whiteness, devoid of color, and you're fairly sure your labors are futile. You're tempted to quit and let fate take its course, but you keep plodding, one foot in front of the other, paying bills, taking tests, raising kids, going to work, doing whatever it is you're doing.

Like the widow, perhaps your dreams have vanished in a puff and you just don't have what you need. Too much is required of you. You can't make the situation work. You've tried, and you've failed.

God shines his spotlight on this hungry little human and asks her to do something insignificant and menial, something for him. He doesn't ask her to pour out a bottle of costly perfume like Mary, preach a sermon like Peter, or plant churches like Paul. He asks her to make a little cake. A little cake doesn't sound so hard, does it? Unless it requires all you have.

It might not be flour and oil that you're running out of. It might be patience. Endurance. Wisdom. Organization. Energy. Love. But God is requiring what feels like your last drops. Sometimes the next small step of obedience feels like a leap across the ocean.

Those small steps are ones that resound in the halls of heaven. They are priceless opportunities to trust that God is at work even when we can't see it. Take the step. Trust God. We will look back from eternity shocked that we ever doubted a record of faithfulness so flawlessly complete.

The widow probably felt very alone in her difficulty, maybe even forgotten by God. When have you felt that way, if ever?

_____

_____

_____

God sent Elijah to this nameless widow. What does this show us about God?

_____

_____

_____

What small steps of obedience is God asking you to take that feel like a leap across the ocean?

_____

_____

_____

BELIEVE

Matthew 10:42: "And whoever gives one of these little ones even a cup of cold water because he is a disciple, truly, I say to you, he will by no means lose his reward."

DAY **3**

Better Promises

Do you tend to be a hoarder or a giver of blessings like money, time, and service? How do God's promises of provision speak to that?

I REMEMBER A FRUSTRATING NIGHT years ago in my college dorm room. As an English major, I was laboring over an analysis assignment of an Edna St. Vincent Millay poem that wasn't cooperating and had become King Kong squeezing me in its fist, turning my brain to jelly. I decided to fold my small basket of laundry as I pondered, but I stopped in the middle. Three towels were folded and two weren't. I sat there like a zombie and my roommate, peeling an orange I can still smell, asked me what in the world I was doing. I didn't know. Those extra towels were just too much for my overtaxed brain. They lay in a heap. We both laughed, but it was a picture of life. I can do this, but that—it's just too much.

Clearly, folding towels does not equate to starving to death like the woman in 1 Kings was. But in both trivial and profound ways, God often calls us one step farther than we think we can go. He asks us to do things we don't think we can do and follow him in ways we wouldn't choose. In a surprising act of obedience, the widow used her last ingredients not to provide for her family but to feed the prophet of God. She did what God asked. A fresh green shoot of obedience sprouted from the soil of faith in her broken heart.

You might remember from today's reading that when Elijah made his request, he also assured the widow that her flour and oil would not run out until God sent rain. You may be thinking, *Well sure, if I had a promise like that from a prophet, it would be easy to do what God asks. But this giant mess with no promise of a good outcome is another story altogether.*

In fact, we have something better. God himself has peppered the pages of his Word with promises—not random ones that we can shake onto our situations like spices from a rack, but purposeful, revelatory promises of who he is from eternity past to eternity future. King, Savior, Father, Provider.

When Paul encourages the church in Corinth to give generously, he reminds them that "God is able to bless you abundantly, so that in all things at all times, having all that you need, you will abound in every good work" (2 Corinthians 9:8 NIV). Writing similar words to the Philippians, Paul assures them that "God will supply every need of yours according to his riches in glory in Christ Jesus" (Philippians 4:19). God's generosity is real, and it fuels obedience. Without a rich, giving God, the widow should scoff at Elijah and keep her ingredients, and we likewise should fight for the most comfortable life possible, filing faith, devotion, and sacrifice away as naive relics of a bygone religion. But if God is who he says he is, his overflowing generosity compels us to give freely, knowing that we will be refilled by God himself. Our oil will not run dry.

Even better than physical food, Jesus offers eternal provision. He fills our empty plates with himself, the bread of life. The same Son of Man who refused the devil's bread in one of our previous studies ensures that his people have all they need. He promises, "Whoever comes to me shall not hunger" (John 6:35). God's care for the widow is yet another detail that points to our need for a Savior, who, ever faithful, kept his word and gave his life for our ultimate fullness in him.

The widow banked it all on a prophet's promise that she would have what she needed. We bank on the eternal promises of God by giving when it makes more sense to hoard. By thanking when it makes more sense to criticize. By serving when it makes more sense to quit. By trusting when it makes more sense to despair. The faith-fueled obedience to do the right thing honors God, proclaiming to the world that the "author and finisher of our faith" writes well (Hebrews 12:2 NKJV).

What little cake is God asking you to make for him from your meager resources? Have you obeyed him or are you stalling?

_____

_____

What does God reveal to us about himself in this recorded event? How should it affect the way we live?

_____

_____

What drives radical obedience? Are there biblical promises you bank on like the widow did?

_____

_____

1 Kings 17:13–16: And Elijah said to her, "Do not fear; go and do as you have said. But first make me a little cake of it and bring it to me, and afterward make something for yourself and your son. For thus says the LORD, the God of Israel, 'The jar of flour shall not be spent, and the jug of oil shall not be empty, until the day that the LORD sends rain upon the earth.'"

And she went and did as Elijah said. And she and he and her household ate for many days. The jar of flour was not spent, and neither did the jug of oil become empty, according to the word of the LORD that he spoke by Elijah.

Trust and Obey

IDENTIFY

What do you complain about most? What would happen if you instead voiced faith or gratitude each time?

THE WIDOW'S NOVEL contained more chapters than she expected. Her current plight wasn't the end after all, and hard as it is to believe, yours probably won't be either. Your bleak view of the future is not God's declaration over you or the ones you love. Speaking from experience, I'd go so far as to say it sounds a lot like the voice of your own fears. You don't need to grieve the end of all things just because this particular chapter is a tough one. Could it be that as we obey God, doing the very next act of obedience it seems counterproductive to do, he is waiting to surprise us with his provision? Maybe we'll see that the patience won't run out. The energy won't run dry. The jar of love will be supernaturally refilled as we obey in faith.

We know that events don't always work out the way we want them to. Sometimes there are last chapters. There may have been other widows in Zarephath who died as a result of the famine. So is it too simplistic to say, "Obey God and everything will turn out all right?" In an earthly sense, yes; but ultimately, I don't think so. When the skies zing up like a window blind and our eyes absorb the bright reality that our hearts believed, we will see that all things, truly, will have worked for the good of those who loved him (Romans 8:28). He will have provided exactly what we needed along the way and to the end. Knowing that now, while we're down here in the turf of our current chapters, helps us trust and obey the God who knows exactly what he's doing.

I lose my grip on God's big promises all the time. When I do, I'm trying to grab the pen from his hands to force in plotlines that back my temporal desires.

I then end up the loser. The widow's human logic (don't give your last food to this mangy prophet) would have kept her from the miracle done on her behalf, and the same is true for us.

Much of life is menial. It rarely feels important and often doesn't make sense. We throw dinner together, study for the test, have the conversation, do what's needed to keep life moving, often with a weary heart. But these actions, carved into the pages of a Godward life, hold startling significance. They matter. The cup of cold water is not forgotten (Matthew 10:42). We really can do all to the glory of God. It doesn't have to feel magical or be accompanied by epic music or be posted on social media and liked one hundred times. We can even whisper prayers when we're doing those hard things: "Lord, make this matter." "Do something with this." "This little cake is for you." Our Father, who hears every whisper, is glad to answer.

When your chapter feels long and the setting looks a lot like Zarephath, ask the Lord how to obey. What would he like you to do? If your heart feels cold and unmotivated, remember that God "works in you, both to will and to work for his good pleasure" (Philippians 2:13). Ask him to help you want to obey, and actually obey. Obedience can even work backward, warming a cold heart and fanning the flickering flame of faith.

Do you excuse yourself from obeying God in particular areas because it doesn't make sense or fit your logic? In what areas?

_____

_____

_____

Which of your menial tasks seems to go unappreciated and unnoticed? Do you believe that God notices and is glorified by them? Ask God to help you live with that in view.

_____

_____

_____

How can obedience work backward, warming a cold heart?

_____

_____

_____

Philippians 2:12–13: Therefore, my beloved, as you have always obeyed, so now, not only as in my presence but much more in my absence, work out your own salvation with fear and trembling, for it is God who works in you, both to will and to work for his good pleasure.

Parallel Stories

IDENTIFY

What small act of obedience is God calling you to do next, and will you trust him and do it in joy?

W HEN MY KIDS WERE LITTLE, they couldn't reach the light switches, so they would jump as high as they could to finally flip the switch and turn off the lights. Sometimes we wish there was a switch we could reach to turn off some of the situations in our lives.

God hasn't provided us with an "off" switch, but we often find ways to mentally quit. Our spaces get messy, our words get sloppy, we avoid what we know we should do, and we feel even worse. Like children, we need to heed the voice of our Father as he lovingly directs and corrects us through his Word and the situations he brings. Are we listening? Obedience shows that we are.

God sent Elijah to warn the people of Israel about their idolatry and call them back to him. He also sent the prophet to an insignificant widow to cure her of her own idolatry and show himself strong. He cares for nations and individuals.

Might the biblical account we've been examining provide an outline for our own circumstances? Follow the parallels: We have a difficult situation to deal with and fear grips us, especially fear for the future. We feel depleted, but God is asking something of us. It might be to trust him by waiting. It might be to act. It might be to just keep going, doing the next thing he's called us to do. But we don't feel like obeying because we're tired and it feels fruitless. We just don't have enough to give.

What we really need is a promise from God.

So very often, when we look to him, our stories continue just like the widow's: we open our Bibles and find that, indeed, God has promised to give us all we need for this very moment, as well as eternal provision in the future. In faith, we believe the promise, get up, do the next thing, and find that though difficulties are still present, our God has been faithful, just like he's always been and always will be. Thank you, nameless woman of Zarephath, for blazing the way. Thank you, God, for speaking to your people and calling us to faith-filled obedience in the most unlikely places.

God writes; we respond. Those are the roles of author and character, and we wouldn't want it any other way. In love, God has written us into his chronicle of redemption, which is infinitely superior to the me-centered tales of our own making. What a privilege to reflect a gleam of his glory as we yield to the author's pen.

Author Paul Tripp writes, "When she went out to pick up sticks for her last meal, the widow of Zarapeth [sic] had no idea of the incredible turn her life would take. It would not be her last day because what was lurking over her wasn't the shadow of death, but the Giver of Life, who would not only give her life, but through her preach life to all who believe. And it all began with a stranger's seemingly outrageous request, followed by an act of faithful obedience."[16]

The Giver of Life revealed his power to the widow yet again in our reading today, raising her son from the dead. In the New Testament, we read of another resurrection that God accomplishes. He raises his own Son and, through that miracle, offers life and joy to not just one human, but all humankind. The Old Testament narratives tremble with the power of the gospel, waiting to burst into life in Jesus. Line after line, they foreshadow our Savior.

God breathes life. His promises bloom. Even though we may not see his whole plan or understand his timetable, we can obey a God like this. Like the widow, when you step out in a small act of obedience, you never know where it will take you. So enjoy the book, the chapter, the sentence, the word, the letter, and the comma you're living in right now. He knows where he's going.

How does your situation parallel the widow's situation?

_____

_____

_____

In what ways do you try to take the pen from God's hands? Do you believe he will work all things for good as Romans 8:28 promises?

_____

_____

_____

How does the resurrection in our reading today point to the resurrection of Jesus? What has God provided for us through Jesus's resurrection?

_____

_____

_____

Hebrews 10:23: Let us hold fast the confession of our hope without wavering, for he who promised is faithful.

TAKE AND SHARE

Even when it doesn't make sense, trust and obey the Word of God. The resources you need won't be found inside yourself but in our generous God, who promises to provide exactly what is best for his people. So look upward instead of inward, and encourage the believers and unbelievers in your life to do the same. In him, every true need is met and every promise fulfilled. You can bank on it.

Behold

A Poet's Reminder

God has surrounded us with reminders of himself. Sometimes all we need to do is lift our eyes from our current problem and look around. His handwriting is everywhere, inviting us to dine at the table of the King.

A Life with No Windows

IDENTIFY

How do the challenges you experience tempt you to go inward, both physically and emotionally?

A FEW YEARS AGO, two artists created a work called "Blind Houses."[17] The exhibit displayed a row of framed pictures of houses with no windows. It was digitally produced, so the homes don't actually exist, but the pictures are strangely unnerving, blank and sinister, like faces without eyes.

It makes sense. You don't see employees fighting for the windowless office or vacationers paying extra for a room with no view. Even early pioneers worked hard to reach the point where they could add crude windows to their sod houses. We're made to look out.

God planned it that way, surrounding us with dynamic artwork. In autumn, our windows frame gold and orange leaves delicately attached to knotty branches on the backdrop of a deep blue sky, and if that bores us he changes the displays each season. If made by man, spectators would stand in mile-long lines to gape at such sophisticated artistry. But I just glance out and notice that the trash can lid blew off.

Christians talk a lot about nature. We sing of peace like a river and sorrows like sea billows. We compare trials to tempests and mercies to mornings, almost like the analogies are programmed into us—and they are. Paul informs us that the beauty around us isn't an accident. Nature's job is to shout truth to our hearing-impaired hearts.

The pressures of life push us inward. We spend more time in our houses, on our phones, in our beds with pillows over our heads. Stress and burdens push us inward emotionally as well, and we stay in our own heads, thinking about ourselves more and more. Instead of locating ourselves in God's big kingdom, we become claustrophobic and shrink Christianity to the size of our own lives, as Paul Tripp says.[18] We lose sight of God, unimpressed by his power, callous to his care, concerned only with the details held in our own sweaty fists.

All the while, gold-dipped maple leaves flutter against the windowpane, invisible breath blows voluminous clouds across the sky, and glints of sunlight shine through branches onto our kitchen tables in kaleidoscope patterns. They testify to "his eternal power and divine nature," and they're obvious enough to be "clearly perceived" (Romans 1:20). Magic only God could make surrounds us, pointing to the Creator who designed everything, but we so often forget to look . . . forget to behold.

God reveals himself fully in his Word and through his Son, but he reveals some of his characteristics through his creation. And he places them as ready reminders to us—if we stop long enough to look.

Notice the intricate flower petal designs of a God whose designs for us are meticulously perfect.

Notice the dying grass that in spring will be raised to life by a God who makes all things new.

Notice the stately trees that point their branches to a God who towers over nations.

Notice the V of Canada geese that are led by a God who loves the insignificant.

Notice the wind that is borne from a God whose imprint is everywhere, even though we can't see him—yet.[19]

David, the shepherd boy, king, and poet of Israel, learned to behold the goodness and provision of the Lord in the midst of great darkness. When the fabric of his own situation was shredding, he saw a larger fabric—the curtain of God's stage—and it changed him.

It would be tough to top David's adversities. He fought lions and hid from a murderous king. He ruled difficult people and fled from a coup led by his son. He experienced the guilt of watching his own arrogant choices devastate the lives of people he loved. He cried a lot. At times he was forsaken, lonely, and ashamed. But David and the other psalmists were people who beheld God in their surroundings. God, in his kindness, has given us a book of their beholdings called the Psalms, which can inspire our own prayers.

What natural "works of art" surround you that point to the reality and glory of God? Do you notice them? Are there ways they remind you of God?

_____

_____

_____

Have you ever thought about the Psalms as prayers to God that you could pray yourself? Open your Bible and try it out.

_____

_____

_____

How might spending more time in God's creation encourage your soul?

_____

_____

_____

Psalm 8:1: O LORD, our LORD, how majestic is your name in all the earth!

Talking Trees

IDENTIFY

In what ways do you want your life to be fruitful?

___

IT WAS A BITTER WINTER'S NIGHT, and I had been in the house with my toddlers for a long time. The floor was a mosaic of Legos, sippy cups, and plastic barnyard animals. My brain was a mosaic of B-I-N-G-O lyrics and random frustrations. It had been a long day.

At one point I stepped out our back door and stood on the cement landing that overlooked our postage-stamp-sized yard. We lived in a duplex, and a chain-link fence separated our yard from that of our neighbors. It was nothing scenic. But it was snowy, cold, and quiet, and without hyper-spiritualizing, I felt the immediate presence of God. In an instant he reminded me, "I'm here. The world is bigger than your playroom. There is a larger reality than the way you feel right now." The Holy Spirit used the night air to refresh my mind, the stars to draw my gaze away from myself, and the snow to remind me of peace and forgiveness. I walked back inside five minutes later—different.

In the very first Psalm, a simple tree reminds the psalmist that there are only two ways to live, and then he reminds us. The person who loves and meditates on God's Word, the writer explains, is like a tree that is planted by a stream. Because its roots are nourished by that stream its leaves don't wither. This tree is green and fruitful even when it's hot as a hairdryer outside and it looks like the tree should wither up into a pile of split ends. The stream of God's Word provides all that tree needs to stand tall and fresh, continuing to grow fruit on its branches.

The godless aren't like that tree. They're like chaff—wheat dust—that blows away in the wind. After a few minutes, it's gone. That's how far our own "truth" and worldly wisdom will get us.

Psalm 1 is why we don't have to quit in hard situations. We don't have to succumb to discouragement or melt in the face of fear, and we certainly don't have to complain about everything that isn't our preference. As we choose to delight in the law of the Lord, his stream will feed our roots, and we will grow, year by year, scars and all, into a people after his own heart. We'll be fresh and green to the end, bearing fruit that not only beautifies our own lives, but provides joy and nourishment to others.

Is there a tree in a nearby park? In your neighbor's yard? On a picture on your wall? Let it talk to you of its Creator and remind you that Christian vitality includes sharing the seeds of the gospel, bearing the fruit of selfless love, standing strong in cultural windstorms, providing shade for the weary, all while reaching and growing ever nearer to Christ.

The created world is not just for poets and philosophers. God gave it to people of all personalities and inclinations, offering us a little taste of his brilliance. When we feel downcast by all that's going on and our soul turns inward, let's go outside and let creation fulfill its intended purpose—reminding us of the greatness and tenderness of God.

How does the tree described in Psalm 1 encourage you?

_____

_____

_____

Do your roots find nourishment in the stream of God or elsewhere? In other words, does God's Word or worldly wisdom more frequently direct your life?

_____

_____

_____

What is one way you could meditate on God's Word in the daytime or nighttime?

_____

_____

_____

Psalm 1:1–3:

Blessed is the man
  who walks not in the counsel of
  the wicked,
nor stands in the way of sinners,
  nor sits in the seat of scoffers;
but his delight is in the law of the Lord,
  and on his law he meditates day
  and night.

He is like a tree
  planted by streams of water
that yields its fruit in its season,
  and its leaf does not wither.
In all that he does, he prospers.

Words That Reach to the End of the World

IDENTIFY

When you spend time in God's creation, what does it speak to you?

OVER THE PAST YEAR, I read a few books written by artsy people—musician, painter, poet—and all of them seemed to do everything well. I enjoyed learning what inspired their creative genius, probably in vain hopes of igniting some in myself. Coincidentally, smack in the middle of each story, the author moved to a house situated in a picturesque landscape. Every last one of them. Basically, they all moved to the Shire. I'm surprised they didn't run into Frodo and Sam puffing on pipe-weed. They planted English gardens and watched bunny rabbits hop across meadows and sipped their tea in the mist of the morning.

It irked me, which is terribly judgmental. But I wanted them to find inspiration in normal settings like the rest of us try to. What if the view from our downtown apartment is a gray warehouse? What if the suburban developer chased away all the bunny rabbits? What if our tea is iced and in a gallon container from the gas station down the street? Is there any inspiration left for us?

In Psalm 19, David says yes, yes there is something for us. It's the sky. We can all find a piece of that, and like all of God's handiwork, it rolls out revelation like an ocean wave, spreading its dancing foam over all that it touches.

What does this have to do with your stressful life? Where is the productivity advice that will get your lists checked off? It's in the sun and the stars. No kidding.

David had a lot on his mind, and he looked up and found God's glory and handiwork hanging in the air above him. The sun spoke of God's daily mercies; the stars shone out knowledge of his majesty. "Their words," David said, reach "to the end of the world" (Psalm 19:2–4).

What message reaches your ears from the distant sparkle of the stars and galaxies tossed into the sky by the hand of God? What song does the sun sing to you in its daily ascension to the sky's cathedral? They are there every day, faithful in their assigned roles, steady in the parts they play, burning for as long as God appoints them to burn.

When your heart is restless and your soul is tired, lay back and stare up at the cosmic mobile your heavenly Father has placed over your bed. Its spheres rotate and revolve. They rise and set. Their lights and colors glow and reflect. Know your Father loves you and will be there tomorrow just as he was today.

David's psalm doesn't end in extolling God's handiwork in creation. He turns to the law of the Lord, admiring God's Word in all its facets, just as he had the sky. It revives the soul, makes wise the simple, brings joy to the heart, and enlightens the eyes. Who doesn't need that? Everyone from mature believers, to baby Christians, to staunch atheists needs God's Word delivered to them in helpful ways. As humanity resides in its God-soaked surroundings, let's live in ways that point to the Creator, testifying that his truth is better than gold, sweeter than honey, and more rewarding than anything else.

God speaks through the world he created, the Word he recorded, and now through his Holy Spirit, who is alive and active in the minutiae of our situations. When a rough situation feels like it's raking the life out of us, creation proclaims God's active, attentive care; the Bible assures us that he will work it all for good; and the Spirit intercedes for us before the Father. There is no need for us to panic with a God like this.

If the heavens' words reach the ends of the world, as David said, what do they say?

_____

_____

_____

Which effect of the law of the Lord listed in Psalm 19 do you need most?

_____

_____

_____

Take a short walk tonight, even if you're tired. Look at the sky and talk to the God who placed the stars. Afterward, record your thoughts on the lines below.

_____

_____

_____

Psalm 19:1–4a: The heavens declare the glory of God, and the sky above proclaims his handiwork. Day to day pours out speech, and night to night reveals knowledge. There is no speech, nor are there words, whose voice is not heard. Their voice goes out through all the earth, and their words to the end of the world.

DAY 4

God's Wagon Tracks

Does the raw honesty of the psalmists inspire you, intimidate you, or surprise you?

GRATITUDE IS MORE THAN A VIRTUE these days; it's its own weird thing. Printed on mugs, journals, notepads, and magnets, it scolds us regularly: "Be grateful!" Generally, this is good advice, as long as our gratitude has an object and we're not just blowing thankfulness pixie dust into the universe in some kind of mindful hocus-pocus.

David had no such pixie dust. As always, he engaged the God of heaven. He lifted his face from his cave or throne or battlefield or wherever he was and said, "Praise is due to you, O God, in Zion" (Psalm 65:1). How often does that statement come out of my mouth in the varied situations of life? David continued by listing God's kindnesses. With joy, he began to count the countless works of God, and his listing became praising. *Wow God, you've established the mountains and stilled the roaring seas. You tell the morning and evening what to do. You water the earth and tend its fields.* David noticed field furrows and rain showers and pastures and valleys and meadows with flocks of sheep, attributing them all to the mighty hand of God. His focus had gone from in to out to up.

Where God travels, life blooms. Verse 11 of Psalm 65 paints one of my favorite images: "Your wagon tracks overflow with abundance." Even God's tire tracks, pressed down in the mud, spring up with the blooms and blossoms of mercy and grace in the wake of his resurrection power.

Bumping along in the back of the wagon, we can't always see it. Sometimes we glance back and see muddy wheel ruts, no life to be found, just tired miles traveled. If we've lived long enough in this broken world, we know the curse has its way for a while, or so it seems.

The Psalms don't avoid this gap between our joyous destiny and painful reality. The second psalm we read today, Psalm 42, is a lament written by one of the sons of Korah, a man who led a rebellion against God. There is no happy legacy here. The writer's lyrics are heartbreaking, his discouragement palpable. His soul hurts. Still, he uses the natural world as a reminder of his place before God. His soul pants for God like a thirsty deer dying for a drink. He feels slammed down by a waterfall, crushed beneath God's waves. He views his surroundings through the lens of his relationship with God.

Though he wonders, like so many of us, whether God has forgotten him, he knows that God is still his rock (v. 9) and he counsels himself: "Why are you cast down, O my soul, and why are you in turmoil within me? Hope in God; for I shall again praise him, my salvation and my God" (v. 11).

In both gratitude and grief, the psalmists engaged with God face-to-face, voice-to-voice, and creation was often the friend that reminded them of who he was. Don't we all feel like our current problems will last forever, plundering all our joy? Our souls need the same treatment that the psalmists' did. Hope in God, little soul. You will yet praise him.

CONSIDER

Like David in Psalm 65, where can you see God's hand in the natural world around you? Train your eyes to notice by thanking God for five of those things right now.

_____

_____

_____

How does verse 11 encourage you: God's "wagon tracks overflow with abundance"? Do you believe God will grow good things behind you as you follow him?

_____

_____

_____

How do you speak to your own soul when you are discouraged? Reread Psalm 42:11. Consider quoting this verse in difficult moments.

_____

_____

_____

BELIEVE

Psalm 42:11: Why are you cast down, O my soul, and why are you in turmoil within me? Hope in God; for I shall again praise him, my salvation and my God.

DAY 5

Be David, Not Thoreau

IDENTIFY

What do you most find yourself looking at, giving your attention to, *beholding*?

I**F YOU REMEMBER** from English class, Henry David Thoreau is famous for his classic, *Walden*. He built a little hut by Walden Pond near Concord, Massachusetts, and bunked there for a year, waxing philosophical about living simply in nature. He wrote about woodchucks and partridges and bean fields and blue ice and nature's power to restore the soul. Like the psalmist, right? Not quite.

Nature's power is its reflection of the glory of the Lord. The most blazing sunset behind jagged mountains is still just a glimpse of his beauty, but that glimpse points us to the great designer himself. The psalmists used nature to remind them of their Creator, and then they ran to him.

Thoreau died fairly young. On his deathbed, someone asked if he'd made his peace with God. "I didn't know we had ever quarreled," he quipped.[20] It's clever but terribly sad. The animals and landscapes he loved so attentively were neon arrows pointing him to God. He missed them, trusting in his shiny new personal philosophies instead.

We can all go theological off-roading if left to ourselves, getting lost in God's gifts of beauty or emotions or friends or relationships and forgetting the one who gave them to us. But Scripture prevents that. Reading the Psalms directs us right back to God. Deal with him, it says. Talk to him. Cry to him. Praise him. Question him. Laugh with him. Scream to him. Sing to him. It's not therapy; it's relationship. Jesus died to bring us to God, and this retroactively applied to David as well. God wants to carry our loneliness and meet us in our frustration. He wants to forgive our anger and comfort our fears. He even wants to loan us his strength to help us accomplish what he's called us to do.

We don't speak to the sky or the stars; we speak to the one who made them, the one who has searched us and known us, who understands everything about us better than we do, who understands what we think, say, fear, and love. In Psalm 139, David again used creation to color his thoughts of the Lord.

He imagines the highest reaches of heaven and the deepest abyss of the sea, infinitely far apart, yet in both those places and everywhere in between, God's strong hand will lead and hold him. He envisions the thickest darkness, reminding himself that it's nothing to God. Getting lost is impossible. God sees clearly in the dark because he himself is light.

The Psalms were recorded for us to pray and sing to God, and like all of the Old Testament, they point to Christ, our great Savior. Jesus sees us in our dark places, stuck in our rooms, under our pillows, hiding when life feels like too much sometimes: too much change, too many scary things, too much work, too many risks. He invites us to look out and up where he's placed shatteringly beautiful reminders of how capable he is of creating beauty from dust. There are swaying trees, marbled stone, shifting clouds, slivers of moon. And then the part of creation he saved till last: us, made in his own divine image.

You do have time to slow down and behold the Lord. Put down the phone. Put down the worry. Step outside. Let the magical air God placed in our atmosphere blow your hair. And start talking to the One who made it all. He loves you.

Does the Lord's intimate knowledge of us in Psalm 139 comfort you or scare you? (A little of both is fine!)

_____

_____

_____

Do you regularly bring your thoughts and feelings to God like the psalmists did, no matter what they are? If not, why not? God doesn't want an edited version of you. Approach him honestly.

_____

_____

_____

Pray Psalm 139: 23–24 to God as you begin your day today or tomorrow.

_____

_____

_____

CONSIDER

BELIEVE

Psalm 139:7–12:
Where shall I go from your Spirit?
  Or where shall I flee from your presence?
If I ascend to heaven, you are there!
  If I make my bed in Sheol, you are there!
If I take the wings of the morning
  and dwell in the uttermost parts of the sea,
even there your hand shall lead me,
  and your right hand shall hold me.
If I say, "Surely the darkness shall cover me,
  and the light about me be night,"
even the darkness is not dark to you;
  the night is bright as the day,
  for darkness is as light with you.

TAKE AND SHARE

If you feel distracted by all that you are thinking about and pulled into your own little world, reread or pray through some of our Psalms this week. Take a walk, beholding the many reminders of God all around you. Enjoy an honest and grateful talk with your Creator. Then consider ways you can share these thoughts with a friend or family member this week.

Settle

A Leader's Craving

An unsettled life requires a changed heart, not a changed situation. In his Word, God reminds us that we'll find the peace and joy we're looking for in him, nowhere else. This week we'll follow Miriam through her many adventures, learning from her experiences that God is always enough.

Walking Restlessly

IDENTIFY

Who do you envy, and what do they have that you long for?

JANE AUSTEN'S CHARACTERS are brilliant because readers see themselves reflected in them, in both fair and foul ways as she might say. Throughout Austen's *Pride and Prejudice*, the haughty Miss Bingley secretly hopes to marry Mr. Darcy, who, maddeningly, is in love with their lesser-born neighbor, Elizabeth Bennet. At her sister's suggestion that Mr. Darcy might marry Elizabeth, "Miss Bingley tossed aside her work and walked restlessly over to the bay window, twiddling its sash, and searching the russet October horizon for signs of life." As the conversation continued, "Miss Bingley's face grew long. 'You are cruel, Louisa, cruel. There is not a symptom, not a shadow of an attachment between Darcy and . . . and that pert, little, sharp-nosed, big-eyed, calculating Miss Bennet!'"[21]

Envy is a unique agony. Craving another's blessing is a disease of the heart that eats us alive while smacking its lips. Proverbs 14:30 says "envy makes the bones rot," an apt description for this common but cancerous sin. Romans 12:15 calls us to "Rejoice with those who rejoice, weep with those who weep." Envy, in rebellion to God's good ways, reverses that command so that we rejoice with those who weep and weep with those who rejoice. Even the well-bred Miss Bingley in her luxurious life of repose became restless and agitated, even cruel under the influence of envy. No human heart is above it.

Why does this topic merit a week's focus in a book about feeling overwhelmed? Because envy's cruel whispers steal peace and contentment and alter the way we see our lives in all the wrong ways. Our cozy apartment becomes a sad contrast to a friend's new house. The retirement package sounds great until the neighbors mention theirs. Our toddler's first words delight us until the younger neighbor kid totters in, speaking in full sentences. And on it goes. Envy isn't picky. Like a raccoon with a garbage can, it can gnaw on anything: our homes, careers, callings, appearance, family, you name it.

The result is that nothing is enough. Nothing feels right. I know I need what that person has and a terrible sad ache spreads through my soul and settles like lead in the pit of my stomach. I need to get, be, or do more, and if I can't, the next best thing is to see what I want taken away from whoever has it. The joy of others-focused love becomes the misery of self-focused lust. So we press on for all the wrong reasons, and calluses of resentment, ingratitude, and discontent grow as we reach for the unreachable. In the process, our bones rot.

Our Lord Jesus Christ is the healer of rotten bones, callused hearts, and skewed vision. He wants to fill our longings with what they were originally designed to enjoy: the wonders of his love. Because repentance is part of that life-giving process, let's not be afraid to examine ourselves, and bring to God the honest version of who we are, which he sees anyway. In him we find forgiveness, renewed faith, and even joy in the struggle. Our sins never outstretch his grace.

Have you ever enjoyed someone's misfortune or resented someone's success? What was it that your heart was trying to accomplish?

_____

_____

_____

Are there ways that envy and comparison contribute to the unrest you feel in this season of your life?

_____

_____

_____

How do the fruits of the Spirit in our reading today counteract envy and rivalry? In what way could you practice love and kindness today?

_____

_____

_____

Proverbs 14:29–30:

Whoever is slow to anger has great understanding,
   but he who has a hasty temper exalts folly.
A tranquil heart gives life to the flesh,
   but envy makes the bones rot.

It Happens to Heroes

IDENTIFY

How much do you enjoy the friendship of God?

HAVE YOU EVER HEARD YOURSELF on video sounding obnoxious and thought, *Oh, please, dear God, don't let me be remembered that way!*

Moses's sister, Miriam, never knew her greatest failing would be recorded for our benefit, but hopefully she would want us to learn from it. Though we'll look first at her most famous flaw, we'll view other vignettes from her life too, remembering all the while that just like we saw ourselves in Miss Bingley, we see ourselves in Miriam.

Miriam lived quite a life. This is the woman whose childhood courage saved the life of her brother Moses as he floated in a basket by the bulrushes. This is the leader who stood close to Moses as he led God's people out of Egypt, between the towering walls of the Red Sea, and through the wilderness to the Promised Land. This is the prophetess who led the nation's women in a song exalting the Lord's glory, serving as an example to thousands in her day, and millions through the Bible's retelling of the story. God used her brothers, Moses and Aaron, profoundly, and he used her as well.

It wasn't enough. Not the prophetic gift, the leadership role, the miracles, the influence, nothing. Miriam let her heart wander from the banquet of God to seek fullness elsewhere.

In his book *Respectable Sins*, Jerry Bridges explains that we tend to envy "people with whom we most closely identify. Second, we tend to envy in them the areas we value most."[22] Miriam identified closely with Moses, and she valued influence and authority. God had given her a lot, but Moses more. That's hard. So she and her brother Aaron discussed this, grumbled about how things were going, maybe rolled their eyes, and ultimately "spoke against Moses" (Numbers 12:1). Commentators disagree on who the Cushite woman was who was part of their complaint, but it is clear that the lava in Miriam's volcano was a craving for Moses's authority. "Has the LORD indeed spoken only through Moses?" they asked. "Has he not spoken through us also?" (Numbers 12:2).

The Hebrew verbs imply that Miriam was leading this complaint session,[23] and God's discipline of her reinforces that view. The most sobering sentence of all follows: "And the LORD heard it" (v. 2).

If we're honest, we've all been where Miriam was at this moment. We may be happily flying our proverbial kite in a field of blessing, but when someone else's kite climbs higher and attracts more attention, things change. Our bright kite staggers, tangling in the trees, requiring another puff of flattery or success to elevate it again. Every moment is precarious and wind-tossed when we are not abiding in God, secure in his love.

What if your heart was so full of gratitude for God's promised inheritance that there was no room left for craving more money? What if you were so amazed that God peeled your dead heart off hell's floor that you had no need for a higher status? What if you were so happy in God's love that you could rejoice in your friend's new relationship or attentive husband? What if Miriam had remembered all she'd seen and known of God for almost a century? Would Numbers 12 have ended like this, with her shut outside the camp?

You may doubt that God can or will fill your cravings. It's true that unfulfilled longings exist in this broken world, and sadness can be an appropriate response. Parts of our hearts will always pine on the soil of this sin-infected planet. There is a holy discontent that longs for the fulfillment of heaven. But don't we too often experience the unholy variety of longing, hungry for the immediate satisfaction of worldly goods or pursuits, ungrateful for what God has given, craving what we don't have?

One of the lessons we learn from this passage is that generation after generation, God's people failed as they followed him, pointing to their need for a Messiah. Another takeaway is that what we think will fulfill us won't. Miriam craved more power and authority, but she already had loads of it. Sin is never satisfied. It leads us along like cartoon characters, dangling this carrot then that carrot in front of us, and we shuffle along, oblivious to the meadows of blessing that surround us on both sides. God made us for more than this foolish and frustrating stomp down the path of discontent. He made us to delight in him.

The Westminster Catechism states, "Man's chief end is to glorify God and enjoy him forever."[24] Far from being a dry theological duty, glorifying God brings an experiential joy and relationship. Knowing him cheers and brightens us. He understands our weaknesses and floods our souls with encouragement. He is the truest friend who crosses the gullies and hills with us on the way to the home he's prepared. If we are humble enough to ask, the Spirit will open our eyes to the glories of Christ, and our temporary disappointments, even the deep ones, will be put in perspective by the comforts of his love.

If God spoke Numbers 12:8 to you, whose name would he insert? "Why then were you not afraid to speak against my servant _____?"

_____

_____

_____

Who are people you identify with who have skills or situations close to yours? How can Christ's love help you love and not envy them?

_____

_____

_____

In what way would strengthening your relationship with God affect envy?

_____

_____

_____

Psalm 63:5–8:

My soul will be satisfied as with fat
and rich food,
    and my mouth will praise you
with joyful lips, when I remember
you upon my bed,
    and meditate on you in the watches
of the night;
for you have been my help,
    and in the shadow of your wings
I will sing for joy.
My soul clings to you;
    your right hand upholds me.

Snapshots of a River and a Sea

IDENTIFY

When you've experienced the greatest moments of joy, were you thinking about yourself or forgetting about yourself?

HEN YOU THINK of family, you probably don't envision a list of adjectives describing them. You think of scenarios, pictures that show who they are. The sibling with the huge laugh. The niece who weaves you bracelets.

The Bible lists God's attributes, but it also shows us pictures of who God is. Miriam lived when some of these biblical photos were taken, and we may recognize her in a few if we look closely. If Miriam had remembered what she'd seen of God as she grew older, she may not have nursed such significant envy in her heart. This week, we'll look at four scenes in Miriam's photo album, remembering the many snapshots of God's faithfulness in our own lives.

The first picture is of a little girl talking to an Egyptian princess. The princess holds a crying baby just lifted out of a basket bobbing in the river. From Miriam's early years, she had seen that God loves to use the humble. He chose her, a poor slave girl, to help save Moses's life. She couldn't have planned that. She hadn't merited a role in Israel's rescue, but God used her in her low-born state. On top of that, God chose her tongue-tied little brother to lead a whole nation to freedom. God isn't wooed by status or talent; prestige doesn't impress him, and he resists pride. Miriam got caught up in the world's game of who can reach the top rung, and she forgot that the greatest displays of glory she'd ever witnessed were 100 percent God's doing.

Your heart may be hungry for more blessing, more adventure, and more love. God offers those gifts in overflowing measure, though they may look different from what you expect. Instead of trying to achieve them through rivalry and self-promotion, step into the adventure of following God in his love and under his blessing. Your need is the perfect receptacle for God to fill. As Bible teacher Nancy Guthrie tells us, "God does his best work with empty, as by his Spirit he fills it with himself."[25]

The next photo shows Miriam, tambourine in hand, leading a throng of women in laughing, shouting, dancing, and exulting the Lord. Behind them, the dark waves of the Red Sea toss wooden chariot pieces like toys—all that's left of the Egyptian army. As Miriam worshipped the Lord for his glorious triumph, she instinctively knew that ultimate joy is forgetting ourselves and celebrating God. It's what we were created to do. Miriam's later envy of Moses turned that around, and she forgot God and celebrated herself. She bowed to her will, honored her name, and promoted her fame instead of God's, and in doing so she reaped the opposite of what she sought.

How interesting that when Miriam glorifies God, we see her dancing among his people, and when she glorifies herself, we find her alone, outside her community. This reinforces a pattern we see throughout Scripture and our own lives as well: Worship God and you'll love others. Worship self and you'll love no one.

When you place selfish goals ahead of God, no upward climb of status or relationship will ever deliver its promise. No stolen blessing will ever satisfy. Conversely, when you live for Christ, no lack or loss can keep you from experiencing true happiness. In other words, the family or love or house or body you don't have doesn't need to mar your joy, and the fact that someone else has what you want doesn't need to unsettle you. It means nothing about God's sovereign and good purpose in your life. Envy is a waste of time and misery. Look at what we know of God through his promises in the Bible. Photos don't lie.

Where in the Bible or in your own experience have you seen God use humble people?

_____

_____

_____

Consider times when God moved in your life, or used you, or filled you with joy in a special way. Were you more aware of yourself or of God in those times?

_____

_____

_____

The last paragraph says, "the family or love or house or body you don't have doesn't need to mar your joy, and the fact that someone else has what you want doesn't need to unsettle you." Why doesn't it?

_____

_____

_____

Hebrews 13:15: Through him then let us continually offer up a sacrifice of praise to God, that is, the fruit of lips that acknowledge his name.

Morning Magic

IDENTIFY

When your heart feels empty, what do you try to fill it with instead of the Bread of Life? Your phone? Friends? Food? Pornography? Introspection? Something else?

WHEN I WAS A LITTLE KID, our family vacations consisted of a week of camping in an open field with some other families. In the middle of our circle of beat-up fold-up campers was a volleyball net, a game of horse-shoes, a fire ring, some bikes propped against a tree, and lots of grass to run around in. Kid bliss.

While roasting marshmallows at the end of the day, one particular dad would constantly tell his kids (my little pals) to settle. If they were fidgety or hyper or whatever parents call it, they needed to "settle." It wasn't unkind, just a word my family didn't use, and it made me laugh. I wasn't sure what settling looked like to him, but it clearly wasn't something his kids ever did.

When we speak of someone settling today, it's usually negative. That girl from college married the loser guy, and she settled. Any job other than our dream job is settling. But settle means "to become quiet and calm,"[26] and sometimes that is exactly what we need to do: settle down into who God is and where he's placed us. Like the psalmist, we need to "not occupy ourselves with things too great and too marvelous for [us]," but calm and quiet our souls "like a weaned child with its mother" (Psalm 131:1–2). We need to breathe. Enjoy. Relax. Settle.

Today's snapshot from Miriam's album is a close-up of dewy grass covered with a thin frost-like layer sparkling in the early sun. Like everyone else, Miriam gathered this sweet, magical manna bread each morning to sustain her for the day. This daily miracle showed her and all the other basket-fillers that God alone was sufficient to lead his people to the Promised Land, and it shows us that God is sufficient to fill our emptiness and meet our needs as well. The Israelites were on a supernatural, miracle-laden camping trip with God as their guide. Like children, they fussed at every stop: *We're tired. We're hungry. We're going to die out here.* And, craziest of all, *we wish we were back in Egypt.* God meets them at every turn with provision, protection, discipline, and guidance.

But Miriam was unsettled. She didn't look long at the miraculous work of God for his people or dwell in gratitude for her daily sustenance. Her envy told her that she needed more, specifically a little more respect and authority. Why was she always second to Moses? Wasn't that sexist? Wasn't that just Moses's ego? She craved something God hadn't given her, and she tried to gobble it up. This sin grieved the Lord, who reigns over all, calling his children to the roles he chooses. Miriam's sin told God his decision was wrong. She thought she knew what the people needed—namely, more of her. Pride is ugly.

If we're restless for something different and discontent in God's provision, we may not be fully trusting God's love. God can make grass grow crackers, so he can surely fill our longings and meet our needs apart from our grasping and thrashing for the gifts we think we need. He has something better for us under the tree.

The physical bread from heaven in Exodus points forward hundreds of years to the spiritual bread from heaven in John 6:35: Jesus the Bread of Life. Manna filled daily needs, but Jesus fills eternal ones, and he does it joyfully, generously, and wholly. Settle down to the banquet table and enjoy the feast.

Like manna, is there a regular provision from God—a sign of his faithfulness—that you don't even notice?

_____

_____

_____

What pictures in your "album" or the Bible's "album" show God's faithfulness to you?

_____

_____

_____

How does envy affect peace in your life? What does it say that you need?

_____

_____

_____

John 6:35–37: Jesus said to them, "I am the bread of life; whoever comes to me shall not hunger, and whoever believes in me shall never thirst. But I said to you that you have seen me and yet do not believe. All that the Father gives me will come to me, and whoever comes to me I will never cast out."

Refreshment from a Rock

IDENTIFY

In what practical ways can you pursue fullness in God when you are tempted toward jealousy?

GOD EXISTS outside of the time he created. To him, "one day is as a thousand years" (2 Peter 3:8). He doesn't see life linearly like we do, but instead he can examine any moment whenever he chooses. Miriam's sad failure doesn't sum up her life. Her envy wasn't all she was, but like all her sins, it was enough to separate her from a holy God. What can be done with the envy that rages and romps through our hearts in defiance of the Lord?

One last picture from Miriam's album gives us a hint. We see Moses amid a sea of thirsty, complaining people, striking a rock and water flowing from it. An odd picture to say the least, and certainly one for the books. Why would God provide water for this riotous mob through the unlikely means of a rod and a rock?

Once again, God was providing for his needy people, but he was also showing us an object lesson, a picture for our own albums. As Moses struck that stone and clean water poured out, he foreshadowed a greater miracle. "Jesus is the true and better Rock of Moses," Sinclair Ferguson explains, "who, struck with the rod of God's justice, now gives us water in the desert."[27]

More than thirsty people need water, sinful people need salvation. Jesus met that most pressing need with his shed blood on the cross, filling our lack with himself. That's the heavenly formula of God's love: he gives and we receive.

If we think life is a lot to handle, the Israelites knew it was. Homeless and sometimes foodless and waterless, theirs were not days at the spa. They doubted. They coveted. They regretted, grumbled, and rebelled. They were unsettled and discontent, made of the same mud as we are. And like us, they encountered again and again a Savior who led them from a land of slavery to a land of promise. There is hope for your unsettled, jealous heart. Jesus has washed it clean to be content in him.

Confessing envy hurts. It's raw and vulnerable, a crashing wave on our sandcastles of pride. But though Jesus resists the proud, he gives grace to the humble, meeting us with mercy and forgiveness and the power to change (1 Peter 5:5). This life that sometimes feels like the wrong one is the exact situation our loving Father has chosen to soften our pride, readying our hearts to conform more and more to the stamp of his image. He does not keep from his children anything that is ultimately for their good.

Miriam learned a painful lesson and experienced God's discipline when she disregarded his truths. But she also saw her salvation foreshadowed as water gushed from that rock. Her stony heart was not too much for the Lord to redeem.

God reminded his people years later through the prophet Micah of his kindness in providing for them: "For I brought you up from the land of Egypt and redeemed you from the house of slavery, and I sent before you Moses, Aaron, and Miriam" (Micah 6:4). God loved Miriam, used her for his glory, disciplined her in love, and remembered her in Scripture.

Nothing will show the world the love of Christ like rejoicing with others' joy and celebrating their blessings, not with gritted teeth but with open hearts expanded by grace. Let's not cater to our envy. Jesus laid down his life for us so that we could confess our sins, receive forgiveness, and enjoy communion with him. God personalized the details of our lives for a reason, and he's glorified when we live them for him. Nobody else's life would be better for you—or your Father would have given it to you—and that settles it.

Look up *rock* in a concordance. Where else in Scripture is God called a rock?

_____

_____

_____

Have you specifically confessed your envy to God, or do you try to call it other less-honest names? Do you believe he will forgive you completely?

_____

_____

_____

Pray for the person who has exactly what you most want right now, and then decide on a small way to express love and care to them.

_____

_____

_____

Isaiah 1:18:

"Come now, let us reason together, says the LORD:
though your sins are like scarlet,
  they shall be as white as snow;
though they are red like crimson,
  they shall become like wool."

TAKE AND SHARE

Where is envy unsettling your heart? Confess the specifics to God and ask him to fill you with the peace and contentment that are only found in him. Enjoy the life God has given you, right here, right now, trusting that he is working in ways that you can't see and that his glory is far better than your own. This is the kind of living that will show the world the heart-changing, soul-filling glory of Christ.

WEEK 8

Trust

A Prophet's Doubt

Disillusionment and discouragement can dampen the brightest of spirits, but Jesus, the Word made flesh, sheds his light on them. This week we will visit a prophet in prison and learn how even the greatest of visionaries needed the Word of God.

It Doesn't Sit Right

IDENTIFY

In what low situation is Jesus waiting to meet you?

LET'S TALK professional sports for a minute. I won't assume the topic is irrelevant in a book written for women. You may love everything about them, or you may live with people who do.

I live with five people who do, but the three males are the craziest. I'm regularly in awe of the sheer volume of commentary careening around the airspace of my home at any time of night or day. Growing up, the topic didn't exist. If I watched a football game on TV before the age of twenty, I don't remember it. Now, it is not unusual for the first words of the day to explode down the stairs: "Did you hear So-and-So got traded?" igniting a firestorm of opinions that could rip the ears off a small child. I know I'll be sitting in the nursing home someday quoting Philadelphia 76ers stats that I don't understand simply because they've been burned into my gray matter.

To be clear, these sports enthusiasts love the Lord, and I love them. My role is the neutral party who offers peace and cookies to traumatized viewers who stumble up the basement stairs after a particularly hard loss. Sports are fickle. They promise the world and then slam your psyche down on the mat in one blow, leaving pessimists disgusted and optimists obsessing over next year's draft picks. It's a study in disillusionment. So is life on earth.

It just feels like situations are supposed to work out. Even with a Bible and pastors who prepare us for suffering, we tend to expect that happiness and success will prance along like two little poodles following us wherever we go. Marriages should generally be happy. Professors should be fair. Children should be obedient. Jobs should be satisfying. Friendships should be easy to make and keep, especially when we're following Jesus. And sometimes they are, and we bask in the breeze of heaven.

But when life doesn't work out the way we expect, it can be disorienting. What did we miss? Where did we go wrong? The garden of Eden seems to be set under "Home" in our soul's GPS, and we can't figure out why we're not ending up there, try as we might. Why all this off-roading? Why the dead ends?

Jesus sees it clearly. He watched earth's shadows deepen as the curse of sin spread its poison from Adam and Eve to all their descendants. He saw us lying dead in our transgressions, so he came to this broken down post-Eden planet to save us. He drank a cup splashing with horrors that should have melted the earth. He died and rose again, inviting us into a new life with new ways. Some of them are surprising, like when he announced to his disciples, "The greatest among you shall be your servant. Whoever exalts himself will be humbled, and whoever humbles himself will be exalted" (Matthew 23:11–12).

This truth, revealed over and over again in the Bible, turns our natural inclinations on their heads. It doesn't sit right in our crooked hearts. If I'm going anywhere, I want to go up, not down. I like raises, compliments, and blue skies, thank you; humility, not so much. Instead of finding peace in the low places where our Savior walks, we often panic in our trials, trying to claw our way out and up as quickly as possible. But God often turns those low places into classrooms, teaching us to trust him not because everything makes sense, but because he is good.

Jesus was born in an animal shed. He was a man of sorrows and a friend of sinners. He had no place to lay his head. He chose a servant's towel over a king's scepter. He was abandoned by his best friends. He was mocked, stripped, and executed in public. He lived a hard life but kept a soft heart, and that humility bore the glory of the gospel.

Jesus wasn't the king people expected, and his kingdom continues to be a surprising one, built on a foundation of humility. Though your Christian life is full of obstacles, hindrances, and hardships, don't be discouraged. In a kingdom where down is up, your disconcerting descent doesn't have to derail you but may turn out to be exactly what God uses to accomplish his good purposes in your life. Lean into the sovereign hand of God. It can hold you.

Are the two verses you read this morning ones you try to live by? Or do they feel off-putting to you?

_____

_____

_____

How is Jesus's lowliness different from what our culture looks for in a leader?

_____

_____

_____

Has a difficult situation disillusioned you? How might the Lord be actively at work in that situation?

_____

_____

_____

Matthew 23:11–12: "The greatest among you shall be your servant. Whoever exalts himself will be humbled, and whoever humbles himself will be exalted."

A Clear Call

IDENTIFY

In what way can you direct people's gaze away from yourself and toward Jesus today?

SEVERAL MONTHS before Jesus came to earth, his cousin John was born. John had been set apart by God and filled with the Spirit while still in the womb, a powerful picture of the dignity of pre-born life and the purposes of God for his children from conception. John the Baptist's assignment was to prepare the way for the long-awaited Messiah, and he crashed onto the scene doing just that. He imaged the Old Testament prophet Elijah in appearance and message, sporting camel's hair and a leather belt, washing down locusts with wild honey, and preaching a prickly message of repentance in the wilderness. An encounter with John the Baptist was not for the faint of heart. His zeal was a lightning bolt that electrified the crowds and singed the Pharisees.

Devotion, not pride, fueled John's boldness. If he wrote a personal mission statement, it would contain three words: *point to Christ*. With inspiring obedience and humility, he prepared the way for the Savior of the world. When people adulated him, he redirected their gaze to Jesus. "After me comes one who is mightier than I," he told the crowd, "the strap of whose sandals I am not worthy to stoop down and untie" (Mark 1:7). When his followers struggled with Jesus's growing popularity, John answered with Spirit-filled joy, "He must increase, but I must decrease" (John 3:30). He understood that the adventure God had called him to wasn't about him. The transient flame of his little candle foreshadowed the true sunlight that had come into the world.

Preaching and baptizing, John anticipated a new order in Christ, a radical break from the way things were. He scandalized the Jewish religious leaders by informing them that being descendants of Abraham, which meant so much to them, meant zilch, zippo. It didn't make them more righteous than anyone else. Their ancestral status balloon was popped and lay in pieces on the ground. God could replace them with stones if he wanted to (John was not one for mincing words). "The axe is laid to the root of the trees," he warned (Matthew 3:9–10). Change is coming. God is doing something new. And he was right! The old covenant would be fulfilled before his eyes, but not in the way that even John expected.

We'll see in the next few days that John had flaws like us. He too had hopes of how things would go, and he needed help to trust God's plan. Nevertheless, his example instructs us. Everyone knew who John the Baptist lived for. Passionate and devoted, he pointed to Christ with his words, actions, and entire existence. Although he was a popular speaker, he deflected glory from himself to Jesus, certain that true life could only be found in the Son of God who had come into the world. He pointed people again and again to the Savior.

We may not be called to preach in the wilderness and eat wild honey, but let's not be too quick to distance ourselves from John's mission. We too can sacrifice a comfortable home for the building of God's kingdom. We can risk looking foolish to share the gospel. We can forgo comforts to serve others. We can rejoice in Christ when our status decreases. We can trust that God will more than make up for any losses we endure. Like John, we can decide that Jesus is worthy of our entire lives and live accordingly.

CONSIDER

How was the new kingdom Jesus was ushering in different from the old?

_____

_____

_____

How do you think John envisioned his mission continuing?

_____

_____

_____

In what role is God calling you to trust him with bold faith? What does that look like?

_____

_____

_____

BELIEVE

Matthew 3:11: "I baptize you with water for repentance, but he who is coming after me is mightier than I, whose sandals I am not worthy to carry. He will baptize you with the Holy Spirit and fire."

Not What We Expected

IDENTIFY

What doubts, if any, have dampened the enthusiasm you had for your Christian calling?

JOHN HANDLED a physically and emotionally taxing life well. He sacrificed comfort, preached truth, and embraced repentance. God gives us grace for big assignments, and it's amazing what we can handle when we feel sure of his call on our lives. The frazzle and frenzy of family life can bring joy to the mom who has prayed for children. Assignments and all-nighters energize a committed young academic. Even the threat of death can inspire zeal in a martyr who loves his cause.

The waves of annoyance and workload and pain make sailing a whole lot more difficult, but they don't necessarily shipwreck us; it's doubt that holds that superpower. The clear call becomes muddled. The vision becomes hazy. *Am I really supposed to be doing this? How can this possibly work out? This isn't what was supposed to happen.*

Even bold John the Baptist who had proclaimed and baptized Jesus was vulnerable to discouragement and doubt, and a dark prison cell didn't help. Herod Antipas had thrown him in prison when John publicly criticized his immorality, and the glowing sparks of John's ministry had been snuffed out and now lay in a heap of dead dark coals. Yes, Jesus was still out there doing things, but where was the new order? The new government? The new kingdom he had preached from his wilderness pulpit? Is this all it had come to? Sure, John had been ready to decrease so that Jesus could increase, but that was assuming Jesus would continue the ministry John had started. A prison cell was not what John had anticipated.

Eventually, John sent his friends to ask Jesus a sobering question: "Are you the one who is to come, or shall we look for another?" (Matthew 11:3). Doubt drips from those vulnerable words, and it's familiar.

We are given one brief life, and as Christians, we long to use it for God's glory. Passionate and full of vision, we are ready to take on the world. "Whatever you call me to, God, I'm up for it!" Those words tumble out while our minds paint a mental picture of what that might look like, often paired with a time line of how events will unfold.

Then the hammer of experience falls, denting our enthusiasm. The projected time line is off schedule, some relational challenges have surfaced, and following Jesus is not the sweet stroll under the willows that we envisioned.

Were we naive to have stepped out in faith with big dreams of serving God? The lifeblood we poured out doesn't seem to have accomplished much. Maybe it was too little. Maybe our whole vision was wrong. Maybe none of it was necessary in the first place. Without obvious results, why continue to plow and sow and water and weed? Why continue to serve and sacrifice? Maybe it would be better to just give up and get comfortable. The mission that used to motivate us overwhelms us, and we wonder if God is who we thought he was. The truth is, God probably isn't exactly who you thought he was. He is infinitely more.

God reveals himself to us in his Word, giving us all we need to know him and please him. But the one who uses earth as his footstool isn't contained by Bible pages or prophetic visions. He is beyond us yet near us, incomprehensible yet accessible, terrifying yet meek, fire yet flesh. John knew Jesus as his cousin and friend, and even believed him to be the Savior of the world. But there was more, much more, going on that John's earthly eyes could see, and so it is for us.

Your moment or season of personal discouragement may feel like a gaping hole in the life you hoped for. But that hole may in time prove to be a window that floods your life with the light of Christ's sufficiency. The Bible informs us that suffering is not outside the hand of God but is used by him to produce endurance and character and hope in the Christian (Romans 5:4). The circumstances we dislike the most are often essentials to our maturing process, helping us see our days with new eyes, enlightened eyes.

None of that makes the process easy. Maturity takes time for prophets like John and for us, but we have a Shepherd–Savior who leads us with patience down the long, circuitous path. "Rather than dispensing grace to us from on high," author Dane Ortlund reminds us, "he gets down with us, he puts his arm around us, he deals with us in the way that is just what we need. He deals gently with us."[28]

Disillusionment will not exist when the veil is removed and we see the Lord face-to-face. We'll see that all we hoped for was true and that the only naivete in play was believing we could do anything on our own in the first place. The strength of God will be on full display. For now, down here in the land of mysteries, we have a brief opportunity to trust God when life doesn't make sense, and we will not regret taking it.

Is there an area where you've lost your enthusiasm for what you are doing? Has the joy of work turned to drudgery? Why is that?

_____

_____

_____

Is it difficult for you to trust God in the low places? What have you learned about God while down there?

_____

_____

_____

How might God want to use your moment of disillusionment or discouragement to show you his sufficiency and encourage others?

_____

_____

_____

Matthew 19:29: "And everyone who has left houses or brothers or sisters or father or mother or children or lands, for my name's sake, will receive a hundredfold and will inherit eternal life."

A Gust of Hope

IDENTIFY

Do you measure your life by your current experiences or the declarations of God?

THE FAITH of brave John the Baptist, alone in prison, faltered. In the darkness he lost his certainty that Jesus was the Christ. But Jesus had not forgotten him. Preaching and healing in towns and villages, the Teacher sent an answer through John's messengers, a word from the very Word of God himself. He said, "Go and tell John what you hear and see: the blind receive their sight and the lame walk, lepers are cleansed and the deaf hear, and the dead are raised up, and the poor have good news preached to them. And blessed is the one who is not offended by me" (Matthew 11:4–6).

His answer sounds at first like a televised news report rather than a word of encouragement, but John would have recognized some of these phrases immediately. Just a short time earlier, Jesus had read similar words from the scroll of Isaiah to shocked synagogue attenders when he began his ministry (Luke 4:17–21). He blew their minds by claiming to be the Messiah.

In this answer, he reminds John of that original vision, that earth-shattering claim. He seems to be saying, "It's me, John. It's all happening, and the prophecies are being fulfilled. It looks different from what you thought, but the new way is here. The Messiah has come. The long-awaited dream is coming true."

What gust of hope must have blown through John's soul as he heard those words! What joy! Maybe there were tears of relief. And maybe there was a small sting as well, as he wished he'd believed what he'd known to be true.

This dialogue between Jesus and a perplexed prophet carries a message down through the centuries to our own ears. It tells us to measure our lives not by our current experiences but by the declarations of God. At the same time John was notching out miserable days on the prison wall, Jesus was saying "among those born of women there has arisen no one greater than John the Baptist" (Matthew 11:11). In both his success and his standstill, John was fulfilling eternal purposes that intertwined perfectly with the grand tapestry of God's plan. Sometimes sitting in the cell is the assignment. May we do it well.

It tells us that our inability to make sense of life doesn't mean it lacks sense. It just means we aren't omniscient and can't yet see what God is doing. Remember Hezekiah and the puzzle pieces in Week 2? God is the one who puts them all together. John saw a vision gone wrong, while Jesus had the end picture perfectly in view and saw that all was going according to plan.

It tells us that God will advance his kingdom in his way, not ours. No one anticipated a "gentle and lowly" Savior, as Jesus described himself later in the same chapter (Matthew 11:29), even though the prophets had foretold it. We humans like success. We like to win, bypassing the lowly parts of life as quickly as possible. But that's exactly where Jesus is drawn, and he tells us in Matthew 11:6 that "blessed is the one who is not offended by me." When our wise Father leads us down an unknown and undesired path, we can veer back in indignation, but he beckons us to follow, never taking us where he hasn't gone before.

Commentator Albert Barnes renders this verse, "'Happy is he to whom I shall not prove a stumbling-block.' That is, happy is he who shall not take offense at my poverty and lowliness of life, so as to reject me and my doctrine. Happy is the one who can, notwithstanding that poverty and obscurity, see the evidence that I am the Messiah, and follow me."[29]

It tells us that disillusionment hits the best of us. John had met Jesus, baptized Jesus, preached Jesus, and embraced the humility of Jesus, and he still struggled with doubt. But instead of ruminating in it, he sent for a word from Jesus himself. If this impressive prophet, commended by Christ, needed the definitive word of God spoken to him in his dark place, might we as well?

Jesus spoke to John's doubt. What parts of God's Word speak to you when you experience doubt or disillusionment?

_____

_____

_____

Do you tend to sit in your discouragement or do you quickly take it to the Lord?

_____

_____

_____

John asked his friends to help him seek Jesus. How do you reach out to others for help when you are struggling? Is there anything that keeps you from doing that?

_____

_____

_____

CONSIDER

BELIEVE

Matthew 11:4–6: And Jesus answered them, "Go and tell John what you hear and see: the blind receive their sight and the lame walk, lepers are cleansed and the deaf hear, and the dead are raised up, and the poor have good news preached to them. And blessed is the one who is not offended by me."

Prying Up the Nails

IDENTIFY

What are three things you love about Jesus? Make a point to think about them throughout the day, and praise him for them as you go to bed.

THE GREAT PREACHER, Charles Spurgeon, said, "Doubt discovers difficulties which it never solves; it creates hesitancy, despondency, despair. Its progress is the decay of comfort, the death of peace. 'Believe!' is the word which speaks life into a man, but doubt nails down his coffin."[30]

I pray with some friends each week, and much of our time is spent prying up the nails of doubt and disillusionment, letting in the warm rays of Christ. The women who come are bright and funny and gifted, but almost all battle unbelief regarding a particular situation in their lives: challenges of singleness or marriage, illness, career changes, struggling kids, and broken relationships, to name a few. We share updates, laughter, and some tears here and there, but mostly we share a need for more of God and reassurance that he is sovereign and faithful.

Like John, when we come to the Lord with our need, we receive his provision. It's usually a scriptural reminder that all God said is still true or a sense from his Spirit that he is at work. Honestly, that's all we need. If his purposes still stand, if he is active in our perplexing situations, if he hears our prayers, if he is a redeeming God, if he rules in love, then all is well. We can lay our situations and mangled hearts once again at his feet.

Do you feel burned out by your assignment in life? Has your vision dimmed? Has the work that used to be delight become drudgery? Do your eyes rest on prison walls instead of sunlit skies? Thankfully, your current perspective means very little about what's really true. Even in uncomfortable places,

God assures us that he is at work, his kingdom is advancing, and we are part of that no matter how limiting our current roles may be. We can praise him while preaching to throngs or dying in prison, while laughing with family or working through conflict, while working as CEO or unemployed. He is with us, and we can bring him great glory everywhere and anywhere (1 Corinthians 10:31).

If that feels difficult, remember that after Jesus sent his message, he informed the crowds that no one had arisen who was greater than John the Baptist, "Yet the one who is least in the kingdom of heaven is greater than he" (Matthew 11:11). Shockingly, that refers to you and me. Though troubles sway our faith, though sin blurs our vision, though we are "least" of all people, we are in reality blessed. In Christ, we have the unspeakable privilege of living in the new covenant of full forgiveness through Christ's blood, and that places us in spiritual terms ahead of the great prophet. Jesus has thrown open the gates of heaven and we can come, not groveling, but running to the Father's open arms, asking for more faith and more courage and more love from his vast stores that are now at our disposal. No earthly jail cell can keep us from God's fields of gold.

Are you struggling to trust God in your situation? Ask the Lord for greater faith. John had to send a messenger, but you can speak to God anytime because of his Spirit living in you.

- Thank God for the countless things he has done in your life. Be specific.
- Acknowledge your feelings of disillusionment. Be honest.
- Confess your pride and desire to have God do things your way. Be humble.
- Ask the giver of all good gifts for greater faith and joy in him. Be expectant.
- Trust that your Father loves you immensely and is with you. Be comforted.
- Believe that all he said is true. Be sure.

No physical or spiritual muscle will produce anything lasting apart from Christ, who takes us by the hand and leads us away from self and toward his glories, which far outshine both the sorrows and joys we experience in this life.

John the Baptist, now rejoicing in the fullness of those glories, did not meet a happy earthly end. In a cruel twist, he was beheaded in prison as part of a royal party joke. But he died knowing that his task was complete, the gospel was advancing, nothing could stop it, and all that the law and the prophets had foretold was—incredibly—coming to pass. In a flash, John flew from the dungeon and stood in the dazzling presence of God, exalting in the surety that it was all, indeed, true.

What does John the Baptist's experience teach us? Does his doubt encourage or discourage you? Why?

_____

_____

_____

How do you think a renewed vision for your life and assignment would change your perspective on all you have to accomplish or endure? Have you asked God for this?

_____

_____

_____

How does meditating on the good news of Jesus change your perspective of what you have to do today?

_____

_____

_____

2 Corinthians 1:20: For all the promises of God find their Yes in him. That is why it is through him that we utter our Amen to God for his glory.

TAKE AND SHARE

Don't let a dark feeling or undesired destination pretend to have authority over your life. Like John, send for a word from God. Open your Bible, ask the Holy Spirit to reenvision you with the truth of your mission, and let "the word that speaks life into a man" pry open the coffin of doubt and let in the light. Share your specific doubts with someone, and include what you know to be true from the Word of God. Then pray together, which will encourage you both.

Ponder

A Girl's Crossroads

God's Word is the plotline that keeps us on course. This week we will hear Mary, the mother of Jesus, respond to her momentous assignment with a Godward song of praise and learn from her as she ponders her place in God's good story.

The Dream and the Reality

IDENTIFY

What assignment in your life feels beyond your ability?

The air tasted of French fries and cotton candy as I stood in line at my town's small fair for a second go on he Rotor, a spinning ride that was probably held together by duct tape. I was ten years old and proud that the Rotor couldn't take me down. I had conquered it and pulled my uncertain friends in line with me, shrugging it off nonchalantly. It was no big deal. I mean, sure, maybe for wimps. Even though it spun so fast that riders suctioned to the walls in bizarre positions and the floor dropped out from under them, my coolness could handle it.

The third time my fifth-grade frame plastered to the wall like a bug on a windshield, the nonchalance began to give way to waves of nausea. I could only imagine where the contents of my stomach would land if it escaped its centrifugal limits. My prayer life ignited in one whirling moment.

Like a kid gasping for air on a carnival ride, we can't always manage life as well as we thought we could. Even things we'd hoped for, prayed for, and stood in line for can become taxing, whether relationships, ministry or career opportunities, or even marriage and motherhood. Instead of thanking God, we find ourselves complaining or calling out for rescue. But carnival rides aside, the proof of a worthy activity isn't always comfort and ease. The Bible is full of real people God called to assignments far beyond their abilities. When that happens to us—and it will—we are perfectly positioned to experience God in new ways.

Jesus's mother, Mary, was taught about a coming Messiah, a future king who would redeem his people and set things straight. Prophecies had said he would be born to a virgin (Isaiah 7:14), and what higher honor could there be than to bear the Anointed One? But it was like waiting for a lottery win. People believed it would happen eventually to someone, but no one knew how it would all end up.

In reality, dreaming about and bearing the Messiah were two very different things. The former was a magical idea, the latter a show-stopping, gossip-inducing, heart-splitting role. But it was the one given to this young teenager highly favored by the Lord.

We can make two mistakes when talking about Mary. Like some religious traditions, we can elevate her to a saintly position as if she were not a sinner, which is unbiblical. But we can also react so strongly to that stance that we devalue her unique role in the birth of our Savior. The Bible presents Mary as a typical human who was chosen by God to carry his Son and exhibited true holiness in her response to God, a response that we do well to emulate. Through her, we should see the extreme love of God who "made himself nothing, taking the form of a servant, being born in the likeness of men" (Philippians 2:7). The reigning Son of God entered a human womb as a one-sixth-inch embryo. Mary reminds us of the depth of our Lord's humility and sacrifice.

We should also note her stirring response to God's revealed will. Mary listened to and trusted the God who handed her this gigantic assignment, which included public shame as an unwed mother and disgrace to her betrothed, along with many other sorrows. The privilege was peppered with hardship, like so many of our own experiences. But Mary knew her call came from the hand of God and that he would be faithful to her. And he was.

What blessings in your life can sometimes feel like burdens? How do you typically respond?

_____

_____

_____

When Mary is troubled by the news in verse 29, how does the angel respond in verse 30?

_____

_____

_____

Reread verses 28–30. How does Mary's response encourage and challenge you?

_____

_____

_____

Luke 1:30–33: And the angel said to her, "Do not be afraid, Mary, for you have found favor with God. And behold, you will conceive in your womb and bear a son, and you shall call his name Jesus. He will be great and will be called the Son of the Most High. And the Lord God will give to him the throne of his father David, and he will reign over the house of Jacob forever, and of his kingdom there will be no end."

Singing Truth

IDENTIFY

Do those close to you more frequently hear you complaining
or trusting God?

MARY'S SIMPLE RESPONSE to the angel's wonderful, terrifying, and life-altering news flattens me. She says, "Behold, I am the servant of the Lord; let it be to me according to your word" (Luke 1:38). One sentence displays faith, wisdom, self-control, obedience, love, devotion, and humility. How did she do it?

We find answers in the song of praise Mary sang when she visited Elizabeth, who was pregnant with John the Baptist in her advanced age. Mary's song, called the Magnificat, displays a breadth of scriptural truth that has left some doubting if it could have come from her. Commentator R. Kent Hughes disagrees. Reminding us that young Israelites were taught to memorize sections of Scripture, he says, "Mary's mind was full of scripture and sacred phraseology from what she had heard both in the synagogue and at home. So when the Holy Spirit came upon her, he took what she had and wove it into this hallowed tapestry. The Magnificat was a poignant, profound divine/human composition, nothing less."[31]

Mary didn't respond to this overwhelming news by assessing how it would affect her personally. She didn't dwell on her fears, projecting them out into the future and following their trail of worry and anxiety. Instead, she placed herself and her situation squarely at the center of all she knew of God through Scripture. She accessed a reality deeper and broader than her own life, from which flowed a faith so beautiful it has been sung and studied through the ages by Bible scholars, children, and everyone in between.

This young woman pondered what events meant in light of the Lord and submitted to his will. She, her parents, and her faith community had stocked her mind with the stories of Scripture, ready to be taken off the shelves when needed to see God's unfolding plan of redemption. Now was that time, and with the help of the Spirit, the volumes were plentiful. Mary wasn't the center of Mary's universe; God was, and so she bowed her heart before him, fixed on who he was.

Among the many rich passages Mary pondered, the first was Hannah's song in 1 Samuel 2, after which she patterned her own song. Mary found a mentor in Hannah, even though she had lived over a thousand years earlier. Like Mary, Hannah dealt with a miraculous and unexpected pregnancy and responded with praise, making much of God. Young Mary had probably memorized that song in her childhood and now used it as a model for her own song, not because Hannah was heroic and invincible but because she too saw that God was more than she'd ever imagined him to be.

It makes me wonder whose songs I pattern my responses after. Do I respond to big assignments from God with songs of devotion or songs of complaint? Songs of praise or songs of self? What do others hear in the tune? More importantly, what does God hear?

Scripture showed Mary a way to process this cataclysmic life change, and in turn, she shows us through the pages of our Bibles. Our situations don't parallel carrying the Savior of the world in our wombs, but they are overseen by the same Almighty God who knows, cares, and ordains the details of our lives. Locating ourselves in the larger scope of his plan is essential for the Christian when life feels like a lot, and giving voice to that truth—like Mary did—will not only reinforce it in our own hearts, but magnify the LORD and encourage those who hear us.

What are the big assignments in your life right now?

_____

_____

_____

Whose song do you pattern your responses after? Are you singing songs of devotion or songs of complaint? Songs of praise or songs of self?

_____

_____

_____

Who in your day-to-day life models godly responses? Who might be looking to you as a model, and how can you encourage that person?

_____

_____

_____

CONSIDER

BELIEVE

Luke 1:46–50:
And Mary said,
"My soul magnifies the Lord,
    and my spirit rejoices in God my Savior,
for he has looked on the humble estate of
    his servant.

For behold, from now on all
    generations will call me blessed;
for he who is mighty has done great things
    for me,
    and holy is his name.
And his mercy is for those who fear him
    from generation to generation."

Picking Up Clues

IDENTIFY

Do you view your life as an individual story or as part of God's larger story? Why does it matter?

SHERLOCK HOLMES, the famous pipe-smoking, tweed-wearing detective of literature, solved impossible mysteries again and again. He did it using observation, patience, and precision, mingled with a spoonful of charming arrogance. He righted wrongs and set things straight simply by noticing what other people ignored. "You see, but you do not observe," he coached his friend, Watson, in one of his cases. "The distinction is clear."[32]

Mary didn't just see the facts of Scripture as historic happenings taught by her rabbi; she "observed" them. They were real to her, clues that laid out God's plan bit by bit until the picture was clear enough to walk by. The news of the God-baby growing inside her caused her to examine those truths even more closely.

Mary saw clues about what God was doing in the story of the exodus, and she sang about God scattering the proud with his mighty arm (Deuteronomy 26:8), just like he did for his people when he led them through the Red Sea and conquered their enemies. She saw clues in the cruel kings that God had overthrown, like the evil Ahab, and the humble servants he had lifted up, like Moses. She knew that God was a just God, a God who would make things right and reverse the wrongs of the world. She saw that he took care of his people, weak as they were, and she knew that he would take care of her as well.

This young girl gripped promises and held on, proclaiming God's mercy "for those who fear him from generation to generation" (Luke 1:50). Where does a teenager find such confidence? Not from her own introspection but from verses like Psalm 100:5 planted in her soul: "For the LORD is good; his steadfast love endures forever, and his faithfulness to all generations."

Mary didn't impress anyone with her status or stature, but her roots reached down through the soil into the river of God, keeping her green and fruitful through the years of tumult that came, even giving her strength at the foot of a cross where her firstborn son hung in love for the world.

The strength to endure didn't come from her, a descendant of Eve like the rest of us. It came from the one she knew and loved, who brings down the proud and exalts the humble, who "has filled the hungry with good things" (Luke 1:53). Mary looked at the scary adventure ahead and assessed her meager resources. Then she looked at the long history of God's salvation project and accepted her role in the master's plan, humbly and happily.

Our loving God observes all we are doing, but we are often not so observant in return. Scripture gives us all we need to know about God's activity, but that requires that we turn from the situation and search his Word, taking another look at the clues he provides. "I confess that I have been blind as a mole," Sherlock admits in a rare moment of humility, "but it is better to learn wisdom late than never to learn it at all."[33]

What truths of God inform your song of response to God?

_____

_____

_____

What parts of the broad story of Scripture would you like to better understand? Ask your pastor or a trusted leader to help you. There are excellent books on the topic as well.

_____

_____

_____

How could you be more observant of what God is doing, looking for clues around you and in your Bible?

_____

_____

_____

CONSIDER

BELIEVE

Luke 1:45: "And blessed is she who believed that there would be a fulfillment of what was spoken to her from the Lord."

Mercies Piled High

IDENTIFY

How practiced are you in going to God's Word to make sense of life?

I **N COLOSSIANS 3:2,** Paul tells us to "Set your minds on things that are above, not on things that are on earth." That's what Mary did in her song. With God's help, she located herself in his wider plan and worshipped him, instead of giving way to understandable panic. She praised God for all he was instead of despairing about all she wasn't.

Praising God is commanded because God is worthy of the loud adulation of every living and nonliving thing multiplied to infinity. He is greater than our wildest imaginings. But we are also called to praise him for our own benefit. Choosing to notice the evident mercies of God and naming them one after another fills our hearts with hope and the reality of his greatness! In both Scripture and experience, God's activity is indisputable.

Life's constant distractions fill our vision like thick clouds hiding the sun. The giant ball of burning gases is blazing and exploding up there in space whether we can see it or not. Likewise, God rules and reigns in glory no matter our perception. We have to remember that truth when the moods and worries and frustrations come. When debt and ailments discourage us. When relational challenges distract us. When funerals grieve us. God has not wavered in any way. The Bible teaches us to ask "What is God doing?" before asking "What am I going to do?" This practice not only puts our lives in perspective, but all of history as well.

Do we locate ourselves in the story of God, remembering the Old Testament adventures of our spiritual ancestors? Do we see their faithful God as our God, their journey as our journey? Do we know that those miracles and covenants were accomplished on our behalf, enfolding us in the epic reconciliation of creature and Creator? Do we follow the finger of the ancient prophets as they point to the little boy whose "name shall be called Wonderful Counselor, Mighty God" (Isaiah 9:6)? Do we heed the words of the apostle Paul in the letters he wrote to churches like ours, encouraging weak believers whose lives were packed with challenges to set their eyes on Christ? Is Genesis our fountainhead and Revelation our ocean?

If so, we can look at our open-ended life and sing because it is hemmed in, behind and before, with a plan exploding with goodness and meaning. God knows us and uses our lives in ways we can't see. Do we trust that our most mundane moments and haphazard interruptions can be woven like golden threads into a project too bright for our eyes to behold on earth?

Mary was given a uniquely significant assignment, but our assignments are God-given too. Our songs can magnify the LORD. Our spirits, while still confused, can "rejoice in God my Savior" because he is worthy of all our praise in every situation. Oh, how these songs of faith please the LORD Jesus, whose Spirit empowers and directs them.

Eugene Peterson paraphrases the last stanza of Mary's song this way:

He embraced his chosen child, Israel;
he remembered and piled on the mercies, piled them high.
It's exactly what he promised,
    beginning with Abraham and right up to now.
Luke 1:55–56 The Message

God has kept, and will keep, the covenants and promises that he made to his people until we see him face-to-face. He's been faithful right up to this minute of your day, and he will be forever. Enjoy your pile of mercies.

In general, is your mind set more on things above or things that are on earth?

_____

_____

_____

As you read, do you locate yourself within Scripture, finding peace from the plan of God? Explain.

_____

_____

_____

What parts of the Bible could you learn more about that would enrich your trust in God's promises and plan? How could you go about that?

_____

_____

_____

Colossians 3:1–4: If then you have been raised with Christ, seek the things that are above, where Christ is, seated at the right hand of God. Set your minds on things that are above, not on things that are on earth. For you have died, and your life is hidden with Christ in God. When Christ who is your life appears, then you also will appear with him in glory.

The Story of God

What is one small way you could weave your intake of God's Word throughout your day?

INSPIRED BY THE SPIRIT and Scripture, Mary sang a beautiful song at a crucial moment in her life, and it's recorded for the ages. But she had many more moments to live out her faith. She surely didn't feel inspired in all those moments, like when she lost the Son of God traveling home from the temple—a just cause for panic! Or when Joseph died, leaving her to parent alone. Or when she watched her son savagely beaten, paraded in mockery, and tortured to death on a Roman cross. The depth of horror in her mother's heart must almost have killed her as well. These situations were all questions for Mary. She must have wondered how all of this could be good or right. How could this possibly be in "the plan" that she had joyfully sung about years before? Had it all gone wrong? Was the dream dead?

Of course, God's good plan was more alive than it had ever been. The climax of his epic plotline was upon her, and yet it looked like it was going nowhere. That's why we can't fully trust what our eyes can see. There is more, much more, going on than we can discern.

In God's sovereign design, Mary was a reflective woman. She thought about all the strange things she had seen—radiant angels and visiting shepherds to name a few—and "treasured up all these things, pondering them in her heart" (Luke 2:19). She aligned her experiences with all she knew about God. That's why we find her in Acts 1 sitting with the disciples in the upper room, praying and discussing the things of heaven. She was a believer. In her pregnancy, she had sung, "my spirit rejoices in God my Savior" and that Savior was her son, now risen and reigning in heaven. The one she carried in her womb had carried her sins to the cross. God had indeed been good, working his transcendent will even in the longest moments of her darkest hours. Now Mary could praise the LORD with an even fuller view of his glories than she had before.

We are invited into the intimate fellowship that Jesus experienced with his mother and brothers and disciples. In fact, as Christians, we have become Jesus's mother and brothers and disciples (see again Matthew 12:50 from today's reading). Somehow, in the wide-reaching grace of God, we enjoy the same spiritual status and love that Mary did. So many benefits of salvation are ours if we take the time to enjoy them.

Our ingenious culture provides countless tools to make us feel like we're in control of our lives: planners and phones and all kinds of helpful devices. Their contribution is real but limited. Functioning on an earthly time line, they deal with days and weeks and a few years at a time, but God's planner is infinite. The tools found in his Word are both eternal and practical, and always accessible.

When you have a lot to sort out, resist instinct. Lay aside your phone and your skill set. Pick up the story of God. Read about who you are in him, what you are called to, and the lengths God traveled to bring you, his beloved, to himself. The good news of Jesus has bearing on every moment of every situation, and it always brings hope. Reading the Word regularly makes these truths familiar and ready when we need them, and it's never too late to start.

Mary pondered the big picture and left with the peace of God. The old hymn instructs us to "Ponder anew, what the Almighty can do, If with his love He befriend thee."[34] Let's consider the LORD Jesus instead of our lists of unfinished business and unsolved mysteries. We will find him to be the truest friend.

What do you think Mary struggled with as she raised Jesus?

_____

_____

_____

What are some things you turn to for vision instead of the Bible?

_____

_____

_____

When do you ponder God's story? How could you build that into your thought life?

_____

_____

_____

Matthew 12:50: "For whoever does the will of my Father in heaven is my brother and sister and mother."

TAKE AND SHARE

Your mind isn't just a task receptacle; it's a tool God has given you to ponder his plans and know him. Studying God's story through the Bible shows us where we fit, reminding us that our life is not primarily about us but about his better, broader story of redemption. Because a big part of that story is welcoming people from every tribe and tongue and neighborhood and nation to find joy in Jesus, who can you reach out to today with the love of Christ?

Gather

A Believer's Lifeline

The demands of life can turn us inward, but God calls us outward to play our part in the body of Christ. A believer's responsibility to gather with God's people is no burden, but instead a privilege of the highest degree that brings unexpected blessings from God.

Elbows Are Needed

IDENTIFY

When have you found that serving or ministering to others refreshed you in a surprising way?

FUNNY BONES AREN'T FUNNY. Whoever named them clearly never smashed their elbows. Maybe they watched someone else do it and thought the resulting hooting and hollering and rolling around on the floor looked humorous. When you accidentally hit that sensitive spot, have you ever noticed that the rest of your body ceases to exist? The only part you're aware of is that melodramatic elbow.

Our Scripture reading today informs us that believers are members of the body of Christ. Christ is the head, and the Bible goes so far as to liken us to body parts: feet and ears and eyes (and I presume elbows as well). When we feel hurt or overwhelmed by a situation, we can be so focused on surviving the hit that we forget we're just one part of an intricate, interdependent body. We forget that an elbow isn't going to get too far without some eyes and some feet.

Needing each other is stitched right into the fabric of our souls by the needle of God. We are designed for dependency, meant to lean on and support each other and spur one another on. Ironically, when we need the church most, we often feel least like engaging. What do we really have to offer in a time when we feel stretched and distracted? Who would notice if we faded into the background? But obedience requires prioritizing God's values even when we're not inclined to, knowing that a design wrought by God from eternity is certainly more trustworthy than the instinct of the moment.

People in biblical times weren't so different from us. Aware that some of the Corinthian church members felt unsure of their place in comparison to others who seemed more important, Paul writes, "If the foot should say,

'Because I am not a hand, I do not belong to the body,' that would not make it any less a part of the body" (1 Corinthians 12:15). He repeats the same illustration with the ear and the eye. Maybe he was picturing specific church members as he wrote. In any case, his God-inspired words assure us that no matter our situation, we are needed members. Separating ourselves not only hurts us, but it hurts the function of the body of Christ. Is there a more serious infraction?

The first nine weeks of this devotional examined the experiences of various people in the Bible, including Martha, Hezekiah, Miriam, and even our LORD Jesus. Here in our last week, the character focus is you, the reader, functioning in God's corporate body and experiencing the grace that comes only by gathering with his people.

Although making time to serve and care for others is counterintuitive when we're busy, it helps us by drawing our vision away from ourselves and our problems (which will never wholly disappear in this lifetime) and toward others and their needs. Playing our part in the church brings needed perspective and highlights Christ's love.

A few years ago, a couple in our church walked through some heavy trials. One difficulty piled on top of another as high as they could see. In the middle of all this, they became small group leaders in a class our church offered that introduces people to Christianity. After the ten weeks ended, the couple asked their pastors to allow them to continue serving in this way because it had lightened their load so significantly. Instead of being a burden as they feared, helping others interact with God had reminded them of God's fatherly care for them. Watching God use their gifts to change others' lives washed them in waves of joy they hadn't experienced in many long dry years.

The answer to stressed lives isn't always adding more serving opportunities as this couple did. Sometimes wisdom is learning to say no or decreasing commitments. But even if we aren't serving in formal roles in the church, God calls all of us to disengage from the spinning tornado of our personal busyness and gather with his people, prioritizing his biblical design.

Do you find that when you have a lot on your plate you tend to move toward or away from the body of Christ, the church?

_____

_____

_____

Have you ever felt like the foot and the ear, wondering if you're really a part of the body? How does this scripture address you?

_____

_____

_____

Why do you think God chose the metaphor of a body to describe his church?

_____

_____

_____

1 Corinthians 12:18–20: But as it is, God arranged the members in the body, each one of them, as he chose. If all were a single member, where would the body be? As it is, there are many parts, yet one body.

A Preschool Picture

IDENTIFY

In what ways do you express dependence or independence in relation to the body of Christ?

GOD'S METAPHOR likening his people to a physical body is jarring. It's so physical, so unexpected, so awkward. Do we really want to be ears and feet? But in a culture that conditions us to put ourselves first and curate our communities to fit our preferences, we could use some jarring. God's way is different and might even sound like foolishness to some (see 1 Corinthians 1:18).

The body of Christ, his church, is a group of physical people with physical laughter and pain. They physically meet together to care for each other and encourage each other to follow Jesus. Christ loves to identify himself with redeemed sinners so much that he unites himself with us in a profound and shocking way: he is the head and we are the body parts, unified to the extreme (see Colossians 1:18). The silliness of an elbow functioning apart from the rest of the human body is exactly what God wants us to see—a ridiculous picture that even a preschooler could appreciate. We are not independent, as much as we like to pretend we are. Not only do we need Christ our head to survive, but Paul says we need the other members of the body as well. Anyone telling us differently needs to go back to preschool.

No part can say to another, "I have no need of you" (1 Corinthians 12:21). This lightning bolt of truth cuts through the haze of self-protection and self-promotion that our world inhales and exhales every day. It cuts through our tendency to judge others as unworthy of our time and evaluate opportunities based only on what we think they offer us.

The iris of a beautiful eye with long graceful lashes may not appreciate the macula, a tiny part of the retina jammed way in the back. But it quietly provides the vision the iris enjoys and takes credit for. The eye is designed to work as a unit, like us. Are there people at your church too awkward for you, shoved too far in the back of your life? Are there folks you deem inferior, unworthy of your time, even if you might not admit it? God says they are indispensable, the very ones you need.

Western culture has always celebrated independence and self-sufficiency, and none of us are immune to its creep into our systems. One of the reasons we may find ourselves stressed out and overwhelmed is because we aren't functioning in the body. We aren't asking for help or prayer or sharing our struggles. We're trying to play all the parts ourselves and looking pretty crazy doing it.

Busyness tells us our schedules are too full to prioritize gathering with believers. Grief tells us we're too empty and that everyone will say the wrong thing anyway. Stress tells us we just need a little relaxation. Pride tells us we can figure it out ourselves. Worry tells us that more thought and time in our heads will figure it out. All are wrong. We need to be connected to Christ our Head and his beautiful body to function efficiently. Invest in his church. Confess your sins. Worship together. Ask for prayer. Love his people. Feel the pleasure of God.

Do you see your need to be connected to the body of Christ? If not, why not?

_____

_____

_____

What excuses do you make for not leaning into Christ's body, assisting in the communal building of his kingdom?

_____

_____

_____

What one way can you increase your commitment to the church that God loves?

_____

_____

_____

1 Corinthians 12:24b–27: But God has so composed the body, giving greater honor to the part that lacked it, that there may be no division in the body, but that the members may have the same care for one another. If one member suffers, all suffer together; if one member is honored, all rejoice together. Now you are the body of Christ and individually members of it.

Ocean Kayaks

IDENTIFY

In what situation do you feel blown and tossed?

IT'S NO COMPLIMENT to be called "children, tossed to and fro by the waves and carried about," as we read today in Ephesians. But God is not in the habit of inflating our egos. The Bible is an honest book that names our problems and offers solutions, and we wouldn't want anything less.

Recently, I learned what it feels like to be literally tossed to and fro when my family got ahold of some ocean kayaks and decided to try them out at the beach. After carrying them to the surf, we jumped in and paddled for our lives. The waves that hadn't looked imposing moments before laughed out loud and tossed us into the air like toys. When we didn't fall out of the kayaks, we crashed down sideways, yelling and laughing and nearly drowning and getting smacked by rogue oars. "Blown and tossed" became physical realities.

They are spiritual realities too. Without help, without teamwork, without scriptural training, we are far more likely to be blown off course doctrinally, tossed into the air, and left paddling in the wrong direction, if not dumped out completely. Because God is committed to our growth, he has designed a structure of care, giving us gifted leaders to shepherd and teach and equip us in his ways.

Maturity in Christ stabilizes us. It teaches us to row in unison, to make progress, to weather the storms together and reach our destination. But maturity is a group project, not a personalized online course. Our Scripture reading today is a picture of flourishing life within the body of Christ. Envision Christians equipped to build up the church, living in unity and learning to know Jesus more and more. They're growing in stature into the fullness of Christ. They're speaking the truth in love; resembling Jesus; fulfilling their roles; and helping the body thrive and build itself up.

The church equips us to be ministers of the grace of God in various ways. This is not a job for the super-Christians, whoever they are, or those with a lot of time on their hands. God calls each of his followers to hone their gifts so they can build up the body of Christ and be built up themselves. Together, God's people contribute to the whole: voices lifted in worship, heartfelt prayers, hugs from friends, faithful preaching, testimonies of God at work, communion cups lifted. Each reminds us of who God is and encourages us to follow him for another week.

God loves to draw us to himself and meet us, as we've seen in previous weeks, but he does so in a unique way when we seek him corporately, shoulder to shoulder with believers who may have nothing in common with us but their love for—and need for—Jesus. Unity like this is otherworldly, attractive to outsiders because it's so clearly borne of God.

When life is complicated, it's easy to fall into complaining or fearing, as if God had wandered away from his throne and gotten lost. God hasn't left us alone. He's placed us in a body where other members encourage us, correct us, mentor us, serve us, counsel us, and we do the same for them. God sows wisdom into our souls through these interactions, but we don't benefit when we hang around the edges. We need to join our brothers and sisters on the inside. The investment will not come back empty. The Holy Spirit who dwells in the midst of his people will reveal more and more of Jesus as he carries us together through the waters to the home he has prepared.

Of the phrases in today's Scripture that describe the church, which encourages you most?

_____

_____

_____

How are you maturing through the gathering of Christ's body? In what area would you like to mature more?

_____

_____

_____

Do you hang around the edge of the body of Christ or view it as optional? Why?

_____

_____

_____

BELIEVE

Ephesians 4:15–16: Rather, speaking the truth in love, we are to grow up in every way into him who is the head, into Christ, from whom the whole body, joined and held together by every joint with which it is equipped, when each part is working properly, makes the body grow so that it builds itself up in love.

DAY 4

READ *HEBREWS 10:19-25*

Stopping a 747

IDENTIFY

Who are you "spurring on to love and good works" (Hebrews 10:24)?

WITH POWERFUL WORDS recorded in Genesis, God created all we enjoy. He is the ultimate source and inspiration for everything. Inventions and new ideas don't take him off guard. The innovative techniques of chefs and engineers don't surprise him. He views the designs of stonemasons with a knowing nod. Even the literary devices that writers employ grew from his fertile mind, including one called irony.

While writing this book about when life is a lot, my life has contained an unplanned and unexpected lot. The irony is not lost on me. Every time I sit down before the manuscript, I encounter the title and grapple with how well or poorly I am applying the principles I'm writing about. But I too need to remember that these chapters and their action points aren't a task list. They simply invite me into a reality that God's saving grace has created for me: the joy of union with Christ himself.

Christ's church works the same way. Gathering with God's people is no mere duty, but a generous welcome to participate in what Jesus accomplished for us in his dying and rising. I need to understand this as I encounter my natural instincts that don't always lead me rightly. For example, the last thing I think of doing when I'm juggling fifty-seven responsibilities is getting together with people. Of course, I do it if it helps me accomplish something or I need social interaction to keep me sane, but the idea of asking a hectic, stressed person to stop for deep fellowship feels like asking a 747 rolling down the runway to stop for a doughnut. Doughnuts are good and all, especially the glazed ones, but it's just not worth the effort. I've accumulated too much speed.

The writer of Hebrews thinks differently in our reading today. Just as he rolls his 747 of massive theological truths about holy places and High Priests down the runway ready to take off into the theological stratosphere, he stops to talk about the church. He transitions his discourse on our mind-boggling communion with God to discuss the gathering of believers, groups of bumbling, sinning humans like us. Can these bunches of regular people really fit in the same passage as supreme revelations? It appears that yes, they can and they do.

As we pursue growth in Christ, we are told to consider one another, stirring one another up, not neglecting to gather but finding ways to encourage each other more and more each day. If we want to look at God, we'll also be looking at each other. Love for God includes love for others. The Father knows his children better than we know ourselves, and he's built dependence into us to ensure that his body functions as it should. We need each other. As encouragement is shared, the leg moves, the foot bends, the arm pumps, and the body moves forward.

Some neglect to meet together, the author of Hebrews acknowledges, and this isn't looked upon kindly. It is not a viable option but a problem to be corrected, like an arm that refuses to work. The body needs its parts functioning together to accomplish its mission.

Part of the reason we feel the weight of our responsibilities so heavily is because we aren't sharing them. It's like one left-hand pinky finger trying to carry a load that other parts of the body are to carry together. I fall into this regularly, standing on my buckling legs and declaring that what I'm lifting is my weight to bear, thank you so much, and I will just have to lift it alone with my cramping pitiful little pinky strength. I wouldn't want to bother you or give you the blessing of honoring Christ by supporting the body. That would be too great a burden.

If we say we follow Jesus, we will follow him to church because we cannot separate him from it. He has made himself one with her and will love her, with all her failings, into eternity. Christ and his church are a package deal.

Who are you spurring on to love and good works? Who are you encouraging today? When is the last time you wrote a note, sent a text, or reminded someone of God's specific love for them? Just as importantly, who are you sharing your weakness with and asking for encouragement?

The irony I mentioned earlier is having its intended effect. This week I stopped the 747 and shared with friends that my fear of man can keep me from talking honestly about all that's on my plate. I confessed this, listened to their thoughts, laughed about some unproductive odds and ends of life, drank coffee, and spent time with the body of Christ. Although no one could do my work for me, a burden was immediately lifted and the encouragement of a few friends changed my perspective. The air was different. I was quicker to sense God and experience his strength. That was not a coincidence but the design of God from the beginning of time. As his body worked together, I sensed his smile.

What is a specific way someone has encouraged you in the past? Who can you encourage in a similar way?

_____

_____

_____

What keeps you from sharing your burdens with others? Should it?

_____

_____

_____

How do you feel about the statement that Christ and his church are a package deal?

_____

_____

_____

BELIEVE

Hebrews 10:23–25: Let us hold fast the confession of our hope without wavering, for he who promised is faithful. And let us consider how to stir up one another to love and good works, not neglecting to meet together, as is the habit of some, but encouraging one another, and all the more as you see the Day drawing near.

The End and the Beginning

IDENTIFY

How does a view of eternity affect your daily choices?

IMAGINE A GORGEOUS FULL MOON glowing gold over the New York City skyline. A worn-out man trudges home, lifting his eyes to the shabby apartment building in front of him but no further. "Look higher!" we silently plead as we watch, eager for him to see beyond the boxy buildings to the beauty beyond. But he doesn't. He misses the glowing orb that casts his whole world in a new light.

Our problem isn't that we look into the future; it's that we don't look far enough. Beyond the uncertainties of the upcoming years lies an eternity of joy for those who trust in Christ. In him, our end is a lovely one—more accurately, it's a beginning. God blazed a trail of mercy that passed through Eden and Egypt and Israel and Bethlehem and Calvary and won us eternity in heaven, free and undeserved. When we spurned God's presence in Eden, he pursued us, revealing himself through the tabernacle, the temple, and then in a manger as a baby born to die. He was crucified on a cross—our cross—and rose again to share his resurrection life with us, signing our adoption papers into God's nuclear family. He loved us from start to finish and will love us into eternity.

Knowing this doesn't remove our struggles here on the spinning planet. Even if the man in our story had looked up and seen the moon, he still had to sleep in his shabby apartment and pay for the subway ride in the morning to get to work. With heaven in view, we still need to make decisions and pay rent and work through relational issues. Loneliness stinks and friends disappoint. Kids have learning disabilities and pain hurts. But the glow of God glistens down on it all, pulling our gaze above the halls and walls of our moments, above the fears and doubts, above the rush and fatigue to take in the invincible promises of God, all a radiant yes in Christ.

Adoniram Judson looked far enough. One of the first American missionaries to travel overseas, he preached the gospel and planted churches in Burma. Faithful and godly, he encountered many hardships, including prison time, the burning of his mission, and terrible family stress. When asked about his hope for Burma in light of these calamities, he replied, "The future is as bright as the promises of God."[35] Judson knew that the church of God would endure whatever came against it, and he lived out of that conviction.

We were made to be part of something bigger and grander than our own brief lives—the body of Christ himself. Grafted into him and sharing the bloodstream of the saints throughout the ages, we are destined to accomplish in Christ what we could never dream up on our own. One day God will make his home with his people, taking his little struggling churches scattered throughout the world and gathering them up in his arms to be with him forever. "The dwelling place of God is with man. He will dwell with them, and they will be his people, and God himself will be with them as their God" (Revelation 21:3).

No better news exists; no better end imagined. Our gathering as the church here, in flawed humanity, foreshadows that great day when God will finally gather us up and fill us with lasting delight. When he will wipe away every tear, and pain will be no more. When life will be a lot for all the right reasons. What a privilege to live in the light of his love, walking hand in hand toward the beautiful end, the fresh beginning, the face-to-face dwelling with God. May the promise of that day light our way.

What do you love about God the most? Tell him now.

_____

_____

_____

How can you lift your eyes more regularly beyond your daily circumstances to your future with Jesus?

_____

_____

_____

Which three weekly themes were most meaningful to you in this book? What small goals can you make to apply what you learned for permanent change?

_____

_____

_____

BELIEVE

Revelation 21:1–4: Then I saw a new heaven and a new earth, for the first heaven and the first earth had passed away, and the sea was no more. And I saw the holy city, new Jerusalem, coming down out of heaven from God, prepared as a bride adorned for her husband. And I heard a loud voice from the throne saying, "Behold, the dwelling place of God is with man. He will dwell with them, and they will be his people, and God himself will be with them as their God. He will wipe away every tear from their eyes, and death shall be no more, neither shall there be mourning, nor crying, nor pain anymore, for the former things have passed away."

WEEK 10

TAKE AND SHARE

The path of independence is a dead end. God calls his children to meaningful participation in a body of believers that build one another up in love. When we honor God by loving his people, we experience the manifold blessings that he has reserved for the church he loves. Inviting others into that fellowship is the natural outworking of our faith, fulfilling Jesus's great command to his followers: "Go therefore and make disciples of all nations, baptizing them in the name of the Father and of the Son and of the Holy Spirit, teaching them to observe all that I have commanded you. And behold, I am with you always, to the end of the age" (Matthew 28:19–20).

CONCLUSION

*We've reached the end of our ten weeks together. Before our paths diverge,
let's review the invitations God gives his children to find refreshment in him.
Christ has died and risen so that nothing stands in our way.*

In the pressing pace of life, choose to **come** to the Savior and sit at his feet to find the meaning and peace you long for.

Spread out the pieces of your unfinished life before the master and **pray** through your problems and heartaches, one by one.

Identify the subtle lies that deceive you, and **fight** them off with the razor-sharp promises of God.

Instead of striving to control your life, **yield** to the God who is true and real and has been leading you all along.

Have the courage to **obey** God in hard places, trusting his mysterious ways and watching him move in power.

When distractions crowd your vision, **behold** the drops of glory that God has strewn before you as reminders of his character.

If your eyes hunger for more of the world, remember God's faithfulness and **settle** into his good plan for you.

Things don't always go the way we hope, so **trust**, even in the disappointments, that God is who he says he is.

Remember the story of Scripture and **ponder** God's ways to find grace for the place God has called you.

We are designed for fellowship, so **gather** with the body of Christ and experience the empowering presence of God with his people.

ACKNOWLEDGMENTS

It's fitting that the acknowledgments come after Week Ten's focus on the body of Christ. The body's members with their varied gifts made this book possible. Dear friends encouraged me, family loved me, pastors taught me, fellow writers assisted me . . . I love doing life together.

New Growth Press, I'm grateful for your investment into this book. Barbara Juliani, Ruth Castle, Dan Stelzer, Irene Stoops, Tara Reed, and Alecia Sharp, thank you for using your talents to make this book what it is.

Thanks to the generous souls who read the draft and offered valuable suggestions and encouragement. Jim, Rob, Davina, Leah, Asher, Meghan, Bryn, Shannon, and Rebekah, this book is better because of you.

Covenant Fellowship Church, you're my home and I couldn't be happier. Most of what I shared in this book I learned from and with you. To the women of CFC, thanks for living out the gospel with joy and faith. You're the real thing. May we enjoy together the welcome of God.

Finally, to my family, I could never do any of this without you cheering me on, propping me up, and laughing with (and at) me. Adam and Bekah, Asher, Bryn, and Shannon—you guys are truly the all-stars. And Jim, this book is for you. As I said in the beginning, you're always my first pick.

ENDNOTES

WEEK 1

1 J. R. R. Tolkien, *Lord of the Rings* (Nashville, TN: Harper Collins, 1991), 32.

2 Psalm 36:5-9

3 "Deep and Wide" was written by Sidney Cox in the early twentieth century.

4 See bridgecourse.org (Glen Mills, PA) for more information.

5 Lois Tverberg, "What was the 'Good Portion' that Mary Chose?" *Our Rabbi Jesus*, September 4, 2012, https://ourrabbijesus.com/articles/what-was-the-good-portion-that-mary-chose/.

6 D. Martyn Lloyd-Jones, *Studies in the Sermon on the Mount* (Grand Rapids: Eerdmans, 1976), 413.

7 R. Kent Hughes, *Luke, Vol. 1* (Wheaton: Crossway Books, 1998), 400.

WEEK 2

8 Jerry Bridges, *The Practice of Godliness* (Colorado Springs, CO: NavPress, 1996), 214.

WEEK 3

9 *ESV Study Bible*, Note on Luke 4:2 (Wheaton: Crossway Bibles, 2007), 1954.

WEEK 4

10 Derek Tokarz, "History of the Ladder" Fixfast USA, May 4, 2016, https://www.fixfastusa.com/news-blog/history-of-the-ladder/.

11 R. Kent Hughes, *Genesis* (Wheaton: Crossway Books, 2004), 361.

12 Catherine Rampell, "The Jim Fixx Neurosis: Running Yourself to Death" *The Washington Post*. https://www.washingtonpost.com/archive/opinions/1984/07/29/the-jim-fixx-neurosis-running-yourself-to-death/681bd977-8295-4d4a-802c-bbfd54684be5/

13 Lewis, C. S., *The Lion, the Witch and the Wardrobe* (Nashville, TN: HarperCollins, 2005).

14 *ESV Study Bible*, Note on Genesis 32:28 (Wheaton: Crossway Bibles, 2007), 108.

WEEK 5

15 Emily Dickinson, "I'm Nobody! Who are you?" Poets.org. https://poets.org/poem/im-nobody-who-are-you-260.

16 Paul Tripp, "The Widow's Gift of Everything," PaulTripp.com, July 20, 2017, https://www.paultripp.com/articles/posts/the-widows-gift-of-everything

WEEK 6

17 Paloma Munoz and Walter Martin, "Blind House: Utopia and Dystopia in the Age of Radical Transparency," LSA Institute for the Humanities, University of Michigan, https://lsa.umich.edu/humanities/news-events/all-events.detail.html/58928-14578364.html#occurrences

18 Paul Tripp, *A Quest for More* (Greensboro: New Growth Press, 2007), 18.

19 Several paragraphs were taken from an article I wrote in the "Together Blog." Trish Donohue, "Look Out Your Window," The Together Blog, September 30, 2019, https://togetherblog.covfel.org/look-out-your-window/

20 Susan Cheever, *American Bloomsbury* (Simon & Schuster, 2007), 168.

WEEK 7

21 Diana Birchall, "Jealousy in July: Who is Jane Austen's Most Jealous Character?" Austen Variations, July 12, 2016, https://austenvariations.com/jealousy-in-july-who-is-jane-austens-most-jealous-character/

22 Jerry Bridges, *Respectable Sins* (Colorado Springs, CO: NavPress, 2007), 145.

23 Nancy Leigh DeMoss, "Remember Miriam: An Example to Follow and a Warning to Heed (Part 1)," Herald of his Coming, from Heart-Cry for Revival Conference, April 2008 at The Cove, Asheville, North Carolina, https://www.heraldofhiscoming.org/index.php/182-past-issues/2008/dec08/2128-remember-miriam-an-example-to-follow-and-a-warning-to-heed-part-1-10-08

24 C. Matthew McMahon, "Shorter Catechism of the Assembly of Divines." *A Puritan's Mind*, https://www.apuritansmind.com/westminster-standards/shorter-catechism/.

25 Nancy Guthrie, *God Does His Best Work with Empty* (Carol Stream, IL: Tyndale Momentum, 2020), 4.

26 "Settle," Cambridge Dictionary, https://dictionary.cambridge.org/us/dictionary/english/settle

27 Justin Taylor, "Keller: Gospel-Centered Ministry," *The Gospel Coalition*, May 23, 2007, https://www.thegospelcoalition.org/blogs/justin-taylor/keller-gospel-centered-ministry/.

28 Dane Ortlund, *Gentle and Lowly: The Heart of Christ for Sinners and Sufferers* (Wheaton: Crossway, 2020), 55.

WEEK 8

29 Albert Barnes' Bible Commentary on Matthew 11:6, Biblia Plus, https://www.bibliaplus.org/en/commentaries/4/albert-barnes-bible-commentary/matthew/11/6.

30 Charles Spurgeon, Sermons 35.455, CH Spurgeon Quotes, quote of the day, April 14, 2022, http://spurgeon.10000quotes.com/archives/150

WEEK 9

31 R. Kent Hughes, *Luke, Vol. 1* (Wheaton: Crossway Books, 1998), 48.

32 Sir Arthur Conan Doyle, "A Scandal in Bohemia," *The Complete Sherlock Holmes, Volume 1* (New York: Barnes & Noble, Books, 2004), 189.

33 Sir Arthur Conan Doyle, "The Man with the Twisted Lip," *The Complete Sherlock Holmes, Volume 1* (New York: Barnes & Noble Books, 2004), 286.

34 Joachim Neander, "Praise to the Lord, the Almighty," Public Domain.

WEEK 10

35 Joe Handley, "The Future is as Bright as the Promises of God," *Asian Access*, August 22, 2019, https://www.asianaccess.org/latest/blogs/from-the-president-blog/1628-the-future-is-as-bright-as-the-promises-of-god.

"Trish Donohue writes with warmth and wisdom, humor and humility. Weaving together stories and biblical truths, her ten weeks of devotions lead us to sit at the feet of Jesus. Are you weary and heavy laden? In this book, you will find rest for your soul."

KATIE FARIS,

Author of *He Will Be Enough* and *God Is Still Good*

————

"I've known Trish for twenty years and have watched her depend on God through life's ups and downs. Over that time, she's cut a well-worn path to the Savior. *You are Welcomed* is an invitation to join Trish on a daily journey to better know and depend on Jesus. I'll be getting a copy for my wife and daughters. I want them to benefit from the biblical truths and wise counsel Trish offers in this beautiful resource."

MARTY MACHOWSKI,

Family Pastor; author of *The Treasure, The Ology, WonderFull,* and other gospel-rich resources for church and home

————

"Life is often a lot, but the encouragement and advice of a godly woman with life experience makes it easier to bear. In this book, Trish Donohue does what the best of friends do: she points us back to God's Word, where we find strength for our souls and courage for our circumstances. Packed with Scripture, these brief meditations will refresh your heart with the gospel of Jesus Christ."

NICOLE WHITACRE,

Coauthor of *Girl Talk, True Feelings,* and *True Life*

"When life feels overwhelming, it's tempting to grit our teeth and try to claw our way out of the chaos on our own. *You Are Welcomed* shows us a better way. Relating common experiences with timeless truth, each devotion lifts our eyes to the God who sees our struggles and is strong enough—and tender enough—to help us."

AMY DIMARCANGELO,
Author of *A Hunger for More* and *Go and Do Likewise*

———————

"As a working mom, I often wake in the morning with a list of things to do and needs to take care of already running through my head. Rarely am I intentional to consider and pursue my own need for refuge, rest, and refreshment. Where do I even start? It's easier to start with the day's to-do list, so before I know it, I'm off and running. Trish Donohue understands the tension we feel and knows the time constraints we're under, and she also knows how much we need Jesus. She gives us an accessible runway to meet with him. Just what we need."

CHRISTINE HOOVER,
Author of *Seek First the Kingdom* and *Messy Beautiful Friendship*

———————

"The Lord of the feast invites us to come. Yet, some of us are strangely slow in our coming. Trish Donohue's book extends a bridge and lends a hand to women who want to think deeply about Christ and their lives of faith. The feast awaits."

IRENE SUN,
Author of *Taste and See: All About God's Goodness*